DREAMS

.....Visionary creations of the imagination.
...... Strongly desired goals or purposes.
.....Something to fully satisfy a wish.
...A condition or achievement that is longed for;
an aspiration.

Dreams come from the Heart
.....As the "Voice" of the Soul.

1

Broken Dreams

By

Everett R. Wood

Second Edition
Copyright 2006, 2018 by Everett R. Wood
All Rights Reserved
ISBN 978-0-692-11492-6

Acknowledgements

...Special thanks to my son, Barry Wood, and my daughter, Kelly Ford, for their help and expertise in the preparation of the book cover, the photo page of the story's main characters, and the story's orientation maps.

... In addition, I wish to recognize my daughter's-in-law, Michele Wood and Cynthia Fravel for their help in the proofing of the story and finding errors previously missed. In spite of all efforts to avoid errors in my first "Literary effort", the final, final review found additional grammatical errors too late to change. With an apology to my English teachers over the years and the more alert reader, I wish to acknowledge these errors and imperfections and promise to do better next time. After all, if it were perfect.... Who, among my family or friends, truly would think I wrote it?

...A thank you, also, to my son, Gregory Wood, for his continuous support and interest in my writing of the book.

...Next, I wish to acknowledge the special understanding given me by all members of my family and close friends, of my obvious obsession I had for this novel and the almost reclusive nature that I entered into during its writing.

Story Preface

This is a historical, fictionalized, tale based on family history and events as related to me by my father Russell W. Wood Sr. and, over the years, by several of his twelve brothers and sisters. The story is about their grandfather, my great grandfather, Robert Wood.

As a young boy, Robert Wood was a serious and idealistic minded individualist. In his teen years, he added an almost overwhelming adventurous and inquisitive trait, which he thought would last a lifetime. Later, he discovered survival itself would bring sadness, darkness and eventually madness. Little did he know his life was to bring him in contact with some great names and events of frontier history.

It became obvious early in my gathering of facts that there was little agreement in describing Robert Wood. Most had known him either as young children or as teenagers. Some described him as "unclean" or "wild looking", while others thought him a "crazy man". After learning the full story, I prefer to think of him as a devoted husband and father who, through no fault of his own, was involved in events that drove him further, ever further, from saneness into confusion.... and broken dreams.

A great deal of research was devoted to this story to assure its historical correctness, as much as possible. However, the knowledgeable reader may recognize errors made or liberties taken with some events, names, dates, or places. It is my desire that those readers forgive my inaccuracies and enjoy it for what it is…. a conjured up story of possible realities based on known family history.

I further hope the story will prompt the reader to think of the scores of other unknown frontiersmen who helped open the American west with their own turbulent and exciting adventures……

-Everett R. Wood-
-Fort Collins, Colorado-
2006/2018

Robert Wood

Photo taken in
San Francisco 1854

Elizabeth Ann Wood

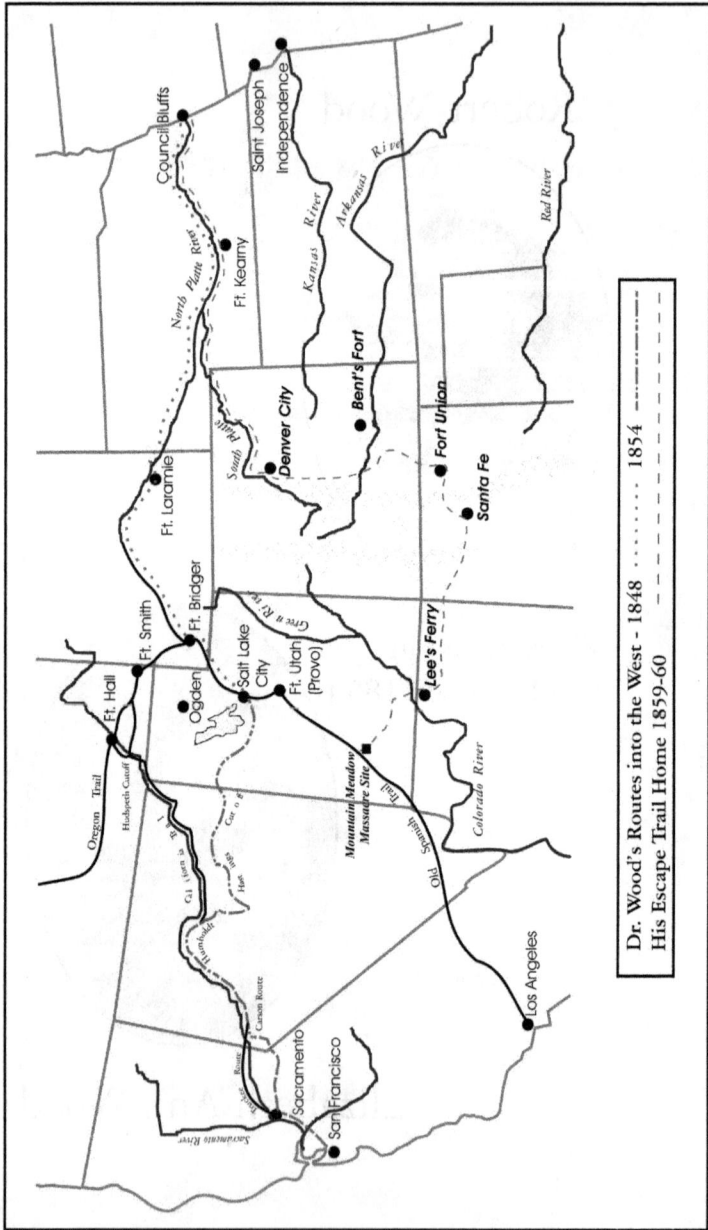

Dr. Wood's Routes into the West - 1848 ·········· 1854 ‒ ‒ ‒
His Escape Trail Home 1859-60 ‒ ‒ ‒

Council Bluffs · Saint Joseph · Independence · Ft. Kearny · North Platte River · Kansas River · Arkansas River · Red River · Bent's Fort · Denver City · South Platte · Fort Union · Santa Fe · Ft. Laramie · Ft. Bridger · Ft. Smith · Green River · Ogden · Salt Lake City · Ft. Utah (Provo) · Lee's Ferry · Ft. Hall · Mountain Meadow Massacre Site · Old Spanish Trail · Colorado River · Oregon Trail · Hudspeth Cutoff · California Trail · Humboldt River · Carson Route · Sacramento · San Francisco · Sacramento River · Los Angeles

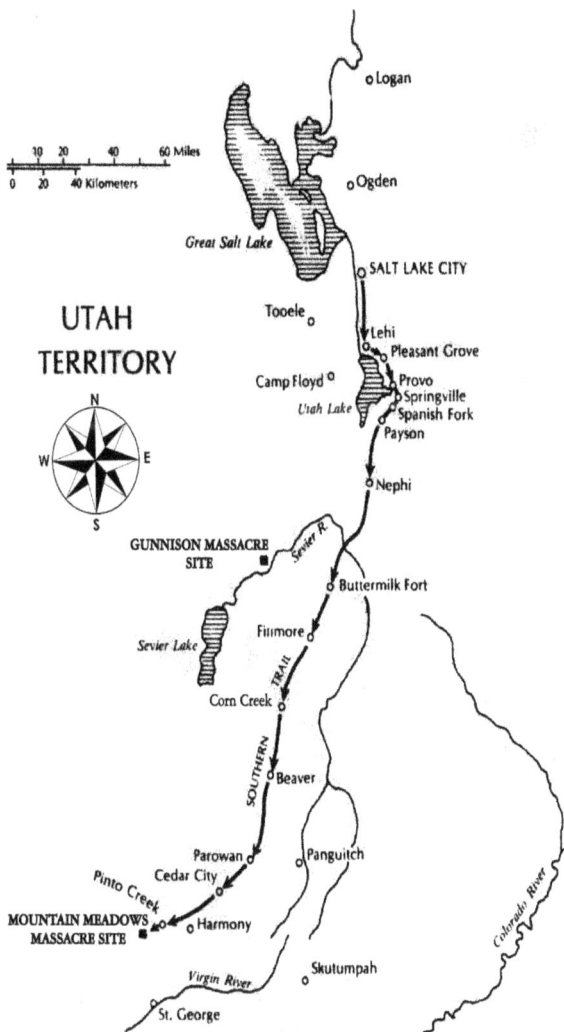

The uncommon and curios area that altered Dr. Wood's destiny in 1848-60

Chapter One

A Promising Future….. 1845

The dismal weather had nothing to do with the feelings they both felt as they topped the last hill of their long journey from Illinois. They looked down upon the town they had elected for their future. Elizabeth gave a quick intake of breath. Robert's face tightened at the sight. It was not a town at all but rather a conglomeration of six or eight homes, if even that.

All Robert Wood and his new wife, Elizabeth Ann, had to start a life in this dreary frontier site was a certificate Robert had received upon his recent graduation from The Chicago Physicians and Surgeons Institute and a seemingly large fortune of $100 that had been given him as a graduation present by his father. A wagon, two oxen, a horse, and a few precious pieces of furniture that had been provided as wedding presents upon their recent marriage.

Their first thought was that they had been terribly misled by various stories of the opportunities to be offered by this new frontier. It was the good Doctor Muir, whom Robert had met at the medical school, who had really been the driving influence in their journey west. Dr. Muir had been a surgeon in the United States Army and sent to the frontier area to protect the Pottawattamie Indians against threatening attacks by the war-like Sioux. He had spent many years up and down the Missouri and he knew the area, this small trading post and its people. He described at length the rolling hills, the beautiful valleys and rich land of the area. Having returned to practice medicine in Illinois after his Army service, he convinced Robert it was sure to grow rapidly in future years, and suggested to Robert that it would be an ideal place to start his new practice.

As their wagon descended the sloping hills toward the "town", the lusty odors of the earth and cattle of community life seeped into their nostrils. A longer whiff of the crisp, clear air of the morning had little calming effect on their first impression of this settlement.

Down the rutted road, they saw what they thought to be a corral with something that resembled a stable. Frank Ragland, the all around stable hand, blacksmith and general handy man, was the first to greet them as they pulled up to the stable. It was his smile and his long curly black hair, just beginning to grey at the temples, which caught Elizabeth's eyes. He reminded her somewhat of her father and she immediately felt more comfortable about their new situation.

After greetings and introductions, Frank inquired about their plans for staying. Up to this point, no thought of the basic need of housing had entered their minds. Frank told them there were two deserted log cabins, either of which might serve their temporary needs. While more fur trappers were returning every day with their winter catches, the fur trappers who had built these two cabins had not returned yet this spring. Such a delay in their arrival hinted at some disastrous encounter during the winter months.

They started down the rutted trail in the direction of the cabins pointed out. As they made a turn around a small hill, they slowed their team of horses at one cabin that Elizabeth thought "Charming!" While this particular cabin was one not called to their attention, they came to a stop to observe it more closely. Almost immediately, they observed a young woman in pioneer garb waving to them from the open front door. As they waved back, the woman began walking toward their wagon to greet them. She introduced herself as Michele LaRouche. This was the start of much conversation and a new friendship.

They learned quickly that where they were was just one of the many fur trading posts along the Missouri river. Louis LaRouche and his young wife, Michele, had been living there for some time. Michele provided the proper name for the settlement as La Cote de Hart. Most, however, just called it Hart's Bluff. Nearby was Mosquito Creek, with its mill that was the main source of supplies for the past few years. Daniel Cottrell and his wife, Sara, ran the mill.

Not long after the Louisiana Purchase from France in 1803, many of the trading posts along the river were established. Just recently, the widely known houses controlled by the Chouteau's, had moved their headquarters up from New Orleans as the town of St. Louis, down river, had become a reality. Other popular trading companies up and down the river were the American Fur, the Hudson Bay and the Mackinaw.

Michele and her husband Louis LaRouche became new "easy friends" of Robert and Elizabeth. Louis was an employee of Chouteau's and very important and popular throughout the area. Through these new friends, they were to meet many of the French Canadian trappers. These trappers were rugged, unkempt men. Some were of French-Indian blood that helped form a connecting link between the savage and the semi-culture of this frontier settlement.

Robert pulled the wagon past the first available cabin, knowing it was in such bad repair that it would not be satisfactory for Elizabeth, even for a short period.

The second cabin sat on a small hill, overlooking the stable area and the cabin of Louis and Michele LaRouche. This would suit them just fine until some other arrangements could be made, or their own cabin built.

As Robert cracked the door open, Elizabeth peeked inside. Where the sunlight stopped and the dark began, something was moving, scurrying around in the darkness that had been interrupted by small rays of light.

"Rats!" she exclaimed, and quickly retreated to safety near the wagon. They spent the first night in Hart's Bluff in the back of the wagon, just as they had done for so many other nights on their way to this new frontier.

So, this was to become Robert's and Elizabeth's home. The start of a nightmare beyond anything they could possibly conceive.

Chapter 2

First introduction to the Real Frontier

A few weeks after they had settled in, the settlement came alive with various activities. Excitement was in the air. A steamship was reported to be down river and heading their way. This was the start of the spring trading season.

Grizzly trappers, Indians and their squaw, began appearing from the surrounding hills and from across the river. The settlement was coming alive. Elizabeth and Robert both shared in the excitement. Neither had previously seen a steamship paddle wheeler. They also were taken by the combination of French "culture", Indian dress and the mixing of various languages. They joined the rush to the river's edge.

With a shrill loud, long, high-pitched whistle, the steamer announced its pending arrival as it came into sight around the last bend in the river. Robert commented to those around them that a band should be present for a proper welcome. With that, the gathering crowd began answering each whistle of the steamship with a volley of echoing guns. The Indians joined in with what was described as war whoops. Even the air seemed to be joining in with a soft breeze, as if encouraging the ship to hurry on its journey up river.

The arrival of the first steamship every spring hadn't changed from year to year. It was the single most important event of the settlement.

As the gangplank lowered to the shore, the crowd, now numbering at least 40 souls, moved forward, each wishing to be the first to greet the new arrivals. With the arrival came news, letters, much needed items, whiskey and money for the pockets of the trappers.

The traders liked the Indian customers the best. They were good patrons, more honest than the whites, and paid their debts more promptly than the whites.

Robert and Elizabeth were enchanted by all the activity and closely watched the process of trading. Both were astonished when one Indian purchased the following: Broadcloth, eight yards of ribbon, pair of stockings, one coffin, saddle, bridle, lard, pins, pen knife, looking glass, sugar, coffee and a parasol. They wondered whom the coffin was for and why the parasol, because they knew no brave would carry around such an item. It was truly exciting to watch.

The activity continued into the night and on for the next four days. It was quite a sight. Indian squaws, in all forms of dress, sitting quietly on log benches, haunch to haunch and the Indian braves strolling slowly, yet powerfully, throughout the settlement. The locals were in their frontier fineness. The traders were dressed in their clean and somewhat elegant outfits. The trappers were dressed in their fringed, dirty, hand sewn leather clothing. All were bartering, talking, and shouting. Mingling with this semi-civilized garb of the frontier were the uniformed soldiers from the nearby small fort.

As was the custom when the trappers got together for this annual event, it was "Tarantula juice" that was the most sought after. Robert was intrigued by the name and soon discovered that it was "homemade". The recipe was as follows:

2 quarts alcohol
A few burnt peaches
A plug or two of black tobacco
Put in a keg and fill with 5 gallons water.

The concoction was most intoxicating and drinkable in spite of personal beliefs. A man would stay drunk for a week after drinking it.

Occasional fights broke out amongst the growing groups of traders, trappers, and Indians. Whiskey and trading didn't mix well.

It was not long before Dr. Robert Wood had his first patient. A knife inflicted wound handed to one trapper by another over a disagreement concerning one of the Indian squaws. Normally, when injury of any sort occurred, a trapper would simply handle it himself. There was no one else to help when in the back country. It was calming to have a doctor now in their settlement. Word that the settlement now had an authentic doctor got around faster than the bullet, which another trapper "caught" somewhat accidentally.

Dr. Wood felt good about opening his physician's bag for the first time since leaving Illinois. His hands were steady and strong as he patched up the first of what he hoped would be many patients to come.   Both of these patients improved quickly and with little after effects. Word spread quickly that the new doctor definitely knew his business.

His third patient was the Indian squaw that had been the point of the knifing the day before. She had been found on the ground, covered in blood, behind Frank Ragland's stable. The Indian braves and squaws that passed had seen her but continued on their way without stopping. It was Frank that found her and immediately carried her to Dr. Wood's cabin on the hill.   The fancy French dress she was wearing had been torn from most of her body, and she had been badly beaten. As Elizabeth began to clean away the blood and cut away the remaining clothing, she wondered who had done this to this poor human. Was it the trappers, the traders, the soldiers, or the Indians themselves who had done the deed? Why had she been dressed this way and who had been responsible for the attack? The truth was never learned.

The girl could not talk, walk or even eat for the first three days. Elizabeth had screened a corner of their "borrowed" cabin for this suffering "creature". A small bed of straw was made for her that had been obtained from the stable. Indian or not, she was a human being, and Elizabeth's proper up bringing would not permit her to turn her back on such misery.

Slowly, the girl improved under both Robert and Elizabeth's care. The question arose what to do with her, as it became time to release her from their care. While it was difficult to judge, she could not have been more than 14 years old, thought Elizabeth.

Her soft, dark eyes, watching from her corner of the tiny cabin, missed nothing, as Robert and Elizabeth went about their daily chores. At first, this made Elizabeth uncomfortable, but she became accustomed to these sad eyes watching and studying her every move. She wished she could communicate with her. If only she knew the language and the girl could speak. She had spoken not one word since Frank Ragland had brought her to them, now two weeks ago.

It was not until Louis and Michele came calling one Sunday afternoon that it was learned that Frank Ragland could speak her language. Robert immediately went and brought Frank to the cabin.

Slowly, softly, and gently he spoke a short greeting to her in her native tongue. Her eyes spoke an inquisitive invitation to him to continue his attempt to awaken her hidden memory. Long into the late afternoon and evening, Frank spoke slowly and clearly, into those watery eyes that began to show faint flicks of renewed interest. Enough for one day! Frank would return tomorrow and continue his efforts to reach and bring her back into her senses.

It became a fascination to Dr. Wood and to Elizabeth as they watched, with patience, as Frank reached further and further into her awakening consciousness. This was to become a life long lesson for young Doctor Robert Wood.

On the third day after Frank's first visit, the Indian girl began to respond. Her voice was halted and weak, but grew stronger with each word she uttered. Soon she told them her name was "Choovio". Frank thought it translated meant "Little Deer" or "Antelope". He wasn't sure since he had not heard the name pronounced exactly as she had done so. From that day on, she was known to all as "Choovio".

Although there was a rather large age difference between the two, Frank become infatuated with her, and as Dr. Wood released her from his care, Frank "adopted" her. It is recorded in history that they lived happily and content in the small cabin by the stable for many years into the future.

So was life on the frontier. Robert and Elizabeth learned quickly that one does not judge, criticize, nor ask too many questions.

Chapter 3

Settling into Frontier Life

New patients arrived at Dr. Wood's cabin during the summer and early fall months. Even some Indians from across the river heard about his "Magic" and came to see it performed. Each case was a bit different and soon Robert felt comfortable in his new practice.

One time he was summoned by the Pottawanimee Tribe from the other side of the Missouri river. He went with trepidation and fear of the unknown knotting in his stomach. He was to attend Chief Wandulta's young son. Thankfully, it was nothing more serious than a childhood case of the measles the boy had picked up from a recent visit with one of the settler's children. However, with the Indians, never previously exposed to such diseases, this could become a full-blown disaster if left untreated and unattended.

Word of his "Magic" began to precede this young doctor on every call. He became concerned that such a reputation could cause false confidence in his limited abilities and knowledge.

Fall began to turn to winter and most trappers had already left with their supply of traps, gunpowder and other equipment for the area beyond the commonly known frontier. Robert's seasonal practice began to wither also, just like the inhabitants. Winter set in with a fury on Hart's Bluff.

Luckily, for them, the trapper who had built and possessed the cabin had not returned along with others this past spring. The cabin became theirs at first snow, under the commonly accepted squatter's rights of this frontier settlement. Had it not been so, Robert and Elizabeth would have been in an utterly dire state. As it was, while his practice had seen a goodly quantity of patients this past season, many had not paid in hard currency as had been hoped. Barter was more basic at this time. Therefore, they had salted buffalo, flour, and heaven only knows how many potatoes, apples and other vegetables now stored a short distance outside their cabin in the root cellar. This, Louis and Frank had told them, would last through the harsh winter if they kept a careful watch out for various varmints that particularly liked to winter inside such root cellars.

The cold frigid wind blew through Elizabeth's skirt as she made her trips to the root cellar and to the well some further distance away.

Each time she attempted to draw water from this shallow, hand-dug, well, she would find a crust of ice on top of the water. She learned from her good friends, Sara and Michele, that it was necessary to drop the water bucket hard down the well a few times each day to assure the ice would not grow too thick. The colder the weather, the more frequently the bucket must be dropped to breakup the forming ice crust. The alternative would be to melt snow for what water was needed.

Trying to stay warm and dry that winter, it became an endless task. But there was little else to do.

Would spring never come again, both Robert and Elizabeth reflected? They had not anticipated this life. Would the next year's spring bring them more security and comfort?

There was no way for them to know that with the first buds of the new spring, great new adventures were in store for them.

Chapter 4

The Surprise

Winter had not been kind. But now a cold, white mist was starting to flow aimlessly off the Missouri River. A sure sign that spring was on its way.

Another sure sign was the increased number of visitors to the Trading Post of Daniel Cottrell and his wife, Sara. Frequent visits to the Trading Post were essential for both ones sanity during these long winter months, and for the latest community news. The locals looked forward to such visits with excitement, in hopes of meeting some of the newer pioneers who had reached the Hart's Bluff area just before the first snow started the winter "hibernation". The late arrivals had settled some distance from the "town" and seemed to prefer to be by themselves. No one seemed to know much about them.

It was on one such visit to the trading post that Elizabeth, with her soft face and friendly manner, became the first to break through their unusual veil of seemingly secrecy.

Two younger women in rather drab dresses had entered the trading post just a few minutes after Elizabeth had arrived. They had looked about fleetingly, as if they felt out of place and seemed anxious to leave immediately. That is when Elizabeth greeted them with a smile and a welcoming comment.

After exchanging a few general pleasantries, Elizabeth learned they were the "Sisters" Mary Jane and Martha. After a few weather comments about the extra cold winter just past, they mentioned their anxiousness to begin with the spring seed planting. "How soon could the planting begin?" they asked Elizabeth.

It was Sara that Elizabeth had to call into the conversation. Elizabeth, being new to the area herself, knew little on the subject. The four ladies retreated to one corner of the store, where they jabbered for the next half hour and would have continued had not a large, burly, bearded man entered the store looking for them. He announced that the broken wagon wheel had been fixed and they now must get on about their deeds. With a hurried short "goodbye" from Mary Jane and Martha, and a quiet grunt from their "abductor", the three hurried out the door.

Early spring planting was not unusual. But it was a surprise when Elizabeth and Sara learned they and six other families had settled on a piece of fertile land in the bottom of the valley near Mynster Springs. More surprising was the amount of land they said they were preparing to plant. Lots of work lay ahead for these people, thought Elizabeth.

It was about two weeks later when Dr. Wood was summoned to the Springs. One of the new young men had struck a large rock with the oxen pulled plow, and had fallen head first onto the rock. He lay unconscious and his head was still bleeding badly when Dr. Wood arrived. Elizabeth had come along mostly out of curiosity.

While the injury of the young man was attended to, Elizabeth sought out "sisters" Mary Jane and Martha. She soon found them, across the field, working side by side with the men who were preparing the field for the planting to come.

The sisters were pleased with the visit and especially for the break in this tedious, tiring work. As they sat in the shade of a big tree, with its damp leaves and lingering smell of winter, their enjoyment of the visit was not dampened. As they talked and laughed together, they enjoyed watching the faint puffs of vapor, which hung over the newly plowed fields below.

The visit and their laughter came to an embarrassing and sudden stop as the same large burly man that Elizabeth had first seem at the Trading Post, approached. It was time to get back to work. "The day was half over and much remained to be done to stay on schedule", they were told. "What schedule?" thought Elizabeth.

As they arose from the damp ground and were brushing off their long skirts, Elizabeth could not help but ask inquisitively, "Who is that man?" Almost in unison, the two young women replied, "My husband".

On the way back to town, Elizabeth and Robert had a lot to talk and wonder about.

Chapter 5

Odd Wagon Train Arrives   Fall 1846

Their wondering didn't have long to wait. In the middle of June, June 14th to be exact, since that was the day Louis LaRouche and Michele had come to dinner, distant sounds could be heard. At first undistinguishable, then, as the sound grew, they thought it sounded like many wagons just over the hill leading into Hart's Bluff. As they looked toward the northeast, they could see small plumes of dust carried over the top of the hill by the evening breeze.

As Louis, Michele, Robert and Elizabeth watched from their vantage point on the hill above the stable, a wagon train indeed began to appear. As it snaked its way down the far end of the valley, they tried to count the number of wagons. At the count of fifty, they became more enthralled with the people themselves as some of the first wagons passed below.

They all looked dirty, tired and weary. Their eyes showed they must have been through some kind of "hell" during their journey. It was all the more surprising that they had arrived out of nowhere.

As more and more wagons appeared over the top of the hill, the wagons seemed to have a predestined purpose and, almost if by divine command, broke into five or six separate trains. Each train headed in a specific, different direction along the river and into the adjacent hills and valleys to seek the area for their nightly bivouac.

The locals gathered at the Trading Post in hopes of learning something about these latest arrivals.   None, however, had any idea who these strange people were, or what they must have been through to make them so seemingly unfriendly and "standoffish". There had been no friendly waves or "Hello's" given in return to those by the locals.

Daniel suggested they all meet at the trading post midmorning next. By then someone would surely have some information to share on these puzzling questions.

Very early the next morning, seven horsemen from the emigrant caravan arrived near the stable in Hart's Bluff. Robert had been up early that morning and was already on his way to the trading post.   As he came close to the gathering, he was beckoned over to the group of men standing nearby. As he approached, he recognized the one who had beckoned. It was the man from the valley up Mynster Springs way who had arrived late last fall.

He introduced himself as Jesse Dunlap and then introduced Dr. Wood to the others in the group.   Robert later was to recall only, "Wagon Master" and "Brother" Black, as it applied to one of the other men. Robert discovered later that Jesse Dunlap was a church elder, with the financial responsibility of the Church.

They further identified themselves as members of The Church of Jesus Christ of Latter-day Saints seeking the "Promised Land" somewhere in the west. Robert thought to himself that this was a mighty big mouth full for a small church.

Jesse said simply, "We're Mormons", as if sifting through Robert's unspoken thoughts. It was then Robert recalled hearing something in the past about such a church group.

As he recalled to himself, it was some sort of a new fangled church that had started in Upstate New York... and something about being persecuted and driven out to Illinois. He held his questions and thoughts. He knew he would learn more as time passed. Robert was not one to jump to conclusions or pass judgments quickly.

Jesse and "Brother" Black seemed particularly anxious to talk with Dr. Wood as they abruptly stopped the "small talk". They exclaimed the caravan of wagons had arrived with injuries, both sustained back in Illinois and along the trail.

While there was a doctor with the caravan, some additional help was needed from Dr. Wood. Some injuries were quite severe and required immediate attention. Robert told them, of course, that he would help any way he could, and asked where these injured individuals could be found. Jesse said he would take him there after the primary business of the gathering had been completed. Robert agreed to get his medical bag from home and then wait for Jesse at the stable where his horse was stabled.

On the short ride north, Jesse told Robert that he was head of the advance party for the approximately 4000 souls who had arrived just the night before in more than 450 wagons. He and his party were responsible for planting crops to help feed the new arrivals. Further, he told Robert that the five groups that had broken off at the top of the valley did so to settle in different locations, which had been predetermined by him.

Each new settlement was to have a name yet to be determined. Names like Florence, Silver Creek, Miller's Hollow and Mosquito Creek had been proposed by Jesse and his advance party. The final names, however, were left up to the new arrivals.

This was the start of an ongoing relationship between Dr. Robert Wood and this group of Mormons.

Chapter 6

Getting to Know Each Other

Robert frequently visited the various new settlements and occasionally, in order to care for them also, would cross the river where another smaller group of Mormons were camped.

The Mormons seemed to look forward to his ever more frequent visits. Robert had found that the Mormons paid for his services in cash, which he needed badly to pay off some debts he and Elizabeth had occurred with Louis at the Trading Post.

The Mormons liked Robert.... And he liked them. Not only for the dollars, he was paid regularly, but equally for their shared beliefs of helping one another, the sick and the frail; of taking care of their own, their apparent gentleness and partly because of the treatment, they had received at the hands of others in Illinois. Vicious attacks had been made on them frequently and had resulted in the deaths of a number of their "Brothers and Sisters". This had happened not far from where he and Elizabeth Ann had departed Illinois a few years previously. He felt a kindred spirit of sorts.

As he treated their illnesses during what the Mormons called their "Winter Camp", he began to learn more and more of these different people. The Elders of the Church began to take an increasing interest in Robert also and would talk to him for hours and hours about their beliefs, their hopes and dreams.

The Church had been started by the Prophet Joseph Smith in New York State. Robert learned about the doctrine of the church, which permitted more that one wife. He learned that the Mormon's views of polygamy served a purpose. That purpose being: one man, ten wives, each having three to five children. In twenty years, the Mormons would be strong enough to protect themselves from the gentiles who wished to attack them for their beliefs. Robert wondered how any man could handle so many wives when he had his own difficulties with but one.

Robert began to spend so much time in the Mormon Winter Camp that Elizabeth barely saw him. While he had shared with her earlier, the substance of what he learned on his visits with the Mormons, she was now much too busy with the cabin and helping Louis and Michele handle the ever-increasing business of the Trading Post.

Their love for each other had not diminished, but they just could not find the time to talk and share things as once they had. This had started to become a significant problem. The less they talked at home, the more time he would spend in the Mormon Camp, listening and talking with them.

As winter approached, their economical condition, while somewhat improved, was not as they had hoped. The extra income and barter credit Elizabeth received from the trading post, and Robert's income from services rendered the Mormons, had all been welcome, but it was barely enough to see them through the winter months. Desperation was setting in once again.

Chapter 7

The Indoctrination Begins in Earnest

As the ice froze over the Missouri river a larger number of the more hearty and daring pioneers moved carefully across the river to the Pottawattamie land, seeking even more fertile land.

The Wood Family spent Christmas day with other Mormons and the Wagon Master, "Brother" Black, and his wife Mary. Elizabeth Ann admitted to herself that she was taken by them almost as much as Robert had been. Simple homemade gifts and jars of various preserves were exchanged. Various discussions were "arranged", very obviously, to discuss membership in the church and the joy of being "Saved". When the Woods finally found a time they could appropriately leave, they were exhausted and their minds awhirl.

The reason they were pushing the good doctor and his wife toward they religion grew obvious. They needed another doctor in their church to care for the membership.

During the "Winter Quarters", as the Mormons called their settlements during this time period, they convened a special council meeting of all the Elders of the Church. Festivities were held a short time later, at which time it was learned that "Brother" Brigham Young had become the second president of the Church, replacing the Prophet Joseph Smith following the martyrdom of him in Nauvoo, Illinois on June 27, 1844.

37

Robert further learned that Brigham Young was doing his part in growing the church with his three young wives, Harrietta, Jennifer and the even younger one, Katherine.

It was also during this period that the settlement became referred to by a new name the Mormons had placed on it. Because of the Winter Quarter council meeting, which had made such important decisions for the Church's future, and because the Mormons were so numerous by now, Hart's Bluff henceforth became known as Council Bluffs, Pottawattamie County, Iowa Territory. The county had been named Pottawattamie after the Indians of the general area and meant "Blowers of Fire" or "Keepers of the Council Fires".

As spring approached, the Elders began to talk to Robert about joining a small exploration group of 143 picked men and women on their "adventure" westward in search of "The Promised Land".

The Church council noted that he and Elizabeth would be well taken care of and they sorely needed a doctor with them since the other doctor was to stay behind to care for the health of the larger settlement. One of the conditions was that they must join the LDS Church.

Both Robert and Elizabeth had expected something like this but were still unprepared. Robert was hesitant about joining, even though he believed in much of their teachings and their doctrines. Robert had not belonged to a church since before he left for medical school, and was too independent in his thinking for such restricted membership requirements of this church in particular.

While the Mormons would have been delighted for Robert and Elizabeth to actually join the Mormon Church, they needed a doctor far more, and began to encourage him to go with them even if he did not wish to become a member at this time. He could join later as he may desire, he was told. This was most unusual since it was not the Mormon's habit to make exceptions. But a doctor they must have.

Chapter 8

To Serve or Not to Serve?   Winter 1846

The closer to spring it became, the more they set out to entice him to go with them. They would call upon him much more frequently than at any time before to come and treat various members of their group. Robert knew many of the problems were minor, and further suspected that many more were faked. Since he was paid in hard currency each time he visited their camp, he smiled to himself and was thankful for their attention to him.

Robert's practice outside the Mormon camp had not improved over the winter months. Other than the Mormon population itself, the growth of the settlement had grown but slightly.

Elizabeth and Robert discussed the option of joining the Mormon caravan as had been suggested. Certainly, this would be, perhaps, the simplest solution to their financial problems, but Elizabeth did not wish to make the long tiring journey that was sure to follow. Besides, Elizabeth Ann was not at all taken with the thought of such a reckless journey into the unknown, as was Robert.

When Robert discussed this quandary with the Elders at the Winter Camp, they quickly saw that they were close to losing him as the chosen doctor for the advance caravan. They must come with a solution quickly since the expeditionary caravan was scheduled to leave less than two weeks away.

The Elders explained to Robert, that while they truly believed in keeping families together, perhaps Robert would consider accompanying the caravan under the arrangements of a special contract. This contract would expire six months after they reached the Promised Land, and then Robert would return home. At that time, Council Bluffs would have grown sufficiently to support more doctors. Additionally, he would be permitted to send money home and stay in touch with Elizabeth by Mormon courier riders who would be returning frequently to Council Bluffs with letters and other news for the families of the Caravan and other Church Elders.

Six months service, plus the length of time the wagon train would take, would mean that Robert would return home early next spring at the latest, weather permitting. He would have sufficient cash for Elizabeth Ann and he to live and enough left over to last them while his practice became further established as the population of the community increased.

This option seemed to be made in heaven. When Robert discussed it with Elizabeth Ann, she was truly delighted for him. While she certainly would miss him dearly, she knew how much both the adventure and doctoring meant to him, and how embarrassing it would be, should they have to return to family and friends they had left in Illinois.

They decided it was worth the year. But he must promise to faithfully forward the money on as regular a basis as possible. This, she said, was the one thing that truly troubled her. To be all alone, with no husband close at hand, was enough to make a person fret. The money the Elders had promised in advance and which would be left with her relieved some of these concerns. This would last her three or four months, and by then the Mormon Courier Rider would surely be back through on his way further east.

Robert was set to accept their offer when he learned some news that made him step back. Elizabeth announced she was pregnant with their first child. While he was disappointed for missing the adventure itself and to experience first hand all that he had been learning about the western frontier from the numerous trappers with whom he had come in contact, he was thrilled with his and Elizabeth's pending adventure of their own. His duty lay with his wife.

The exploratory wagon train left on April 17, 1846 with the one hundred and forty three individuals that had been hand picked by the new Prophet, Brigham Young himself. The wagon train left on schedule in search of the "Promised Land", but without Dr. Robert Wood who they had hoped would be accompanying them.

The greater disappointment was Elizabeth's miscarriage in late April. She had been doing too much heavy work at the trading post in preparation for the early return of the fur trappers.

Rather than the event being overly depressing to her, the dormant sexuality of her body awakened. Her reactions surprised, but pleased, both she and Robert. Her femininity responded to his masculinity and she was pregnant again before the first of July.

It was on October 31 that Brigham Young and "Brother" Black returned with but half of the people he had left with just 6 months before. "The Promised Land" had been found. Preparations must be made for the exodus early next spring from the Council Bluff's settlements to this newly discovered land. The settlement became jubilant with uncontrolled excitement, seemingly ready to explode in anticipation.

Chapter 9

Out of Necessity…. 1848

Elizabeth and Robert's son, George Adelbert Wood, was born in the spring, on March 4, 1848 to be exact, with no complication. The midwife Robert had been training the last 1½ years was again invaluable. Robert was delighted, almost euphoric, about the birth of his first born son. But reality soon set in. With one more mouth to feed, it was going to be even more difficult.

During the entire winter months, the settlement had continued to celebrate and prepare for their final journey west to the "Promised Land". Robert continued to contemplate what such an exodus would do to his medical practice.

On various visits to the stable to visit with Frank Ragland and his Indian "Bride", Choovio, or to the trading post, he frequently exchanged greetings with both "Brother" Black and Jesse Dunlap. After one such visit, he retired to the back room of the small trading post for coffee with his good friend Louis LaRouche. It was Louis that pointed out to Robert that it was obvious that the campaign to attract Robert to the Church and to their needs was again on and reaching new proportions. Hadn't Robert noticed, Louis inquired? Robert admitted that he had begun to feel some new pressure being applied.

When he returned to his cabin on the hill, he spoke with Elizabeth about the casual comments that obviously were again being "dropped his way" by the Mormon Elders.

During that afternoon, only interrupted by the baby's urgent cries, they discussed various options just as they had done many times before.   Again, they came to a similar conclusion. Even with their new son, George only a month old, they both agreed it would be best for their family's future prosperity that Robert follow the opportunity, which had previously been presented. Robert, however, was to seek a shorter contract than the year that previously had been proposed.

The very next morning he sent word to President Brigham Young seeking an audience with him, "Brother" Black and Jesse Dunlap. The request was answered quickly, with an audience set up for the following mid afternoon.

Robert, dressed in a heavy wool coat and scarf against an early spring winter extension, set off on horseback to be punctual for this important audience. He had met Brigham Young only once before and had found him to be a rather stern, unfriendly and distant individual.

In preparation, Robert permitted his mind to consider the various details that would probably arise   during   the meeting.   The chill most would have felt this spring day, was not felt by Robert as he rode briskly toward his "future".

Even though the surrounding area now had over 1000 cabins with an estimated population of 5000 to 6000, everyone in the expanding settlement knew exactly where Elder Young lived.   It was not easily missed with its 70 or 80-foot tall flagpole, which stood in front of his more elegant cabin. The flagpole flew the flag of the Church of the Latter Day Saints, not that of the expanding United States of America.

All three, "Brother" Black, Jesse Dunlap and Robert, arrived within minutes of each other.

They entered Brigham Young's cabin together. A well-kept cabin, thought Robert, but why not, with three "wives" attending it. It was Harrietta, Young's wife #1, which seated the group and immediately brought each a glass of fresh water.

The arbitration was nothing like Robert had conjured up on his ride over. It was brief and to the point. A contract was struck.

The contract was a very simple one: Doctor Robert Wood would leave with the next wagon train. The contract would expire four months after the day of departure, at which time Robert could return home. He would travel in the wagon yet to be assigned. It was agreed Elizabeth and their new son would remain in Council Bluffs. If he elected to stay longer, he would be permitted to send money home with the Mormon courier riders who would be returning frequently to Council Bluffs and beyond. Additionally, he would be given a sturdy horse for his return home.

A formal contract, short and sweet, was drawn up by Jesse as the financial head of the Church. It was signed by Young, Dunlap and Robert Wood and further witnessed by "Brother" Black and Harrietta Young. It became official before three p.m. that afternoon. Robert joyfully set off for his return trip home with the contract in his coat pocket.

Elizabeth was waiting expectantly at the door of their cabin as he rode up with a big smile on his face. She knew instantly that the deed had been accomplished and all to their joint expectations. Four months service plus perhaps a little extra, would mean that Robert would return home sometime in the early fall, weather permitting.

Little had the two of them anticipated that the "next wagon train" would be leaving in just a little over two weeks.

45

Chapter 10

The Parting.......

Robert and Elizabeth invited Louis and Michele to join them for a celebration of their anticipated good fortune. A jug of the infamous "Tarantula Juice" arrived with Louis at 6 o'clock, all hoping it would last the evening and that they would survive another entanglement with such a wild concoction. After the second glass, Robert began to express lingering doubt about what he had done. His new son.... leaving Elizabeth with the sole responsibility.... concerns about assuring her continued health after George Adelbert's birth such a short time ago.... his concerns for the patients he would be leaving without proper health care.... All this produced a creeping uneasiness at the bottom of his heart.

These concerns were of little importance, Michele told them. She assured them both that she and Louis would watch over the family in the true frontier manner and they should worry any further. Also, just that day, she had learned a new doctor and his wife had arrived in the settlement from Missouri. Surely, both Elizabeth and the few patients Dr. Wood was leaving behind would be cared for very well.

After the third or fourth glass of "Tarantula Juice", it was agreed that there really was no problem that could not be handled in Robert's absence. With the fifth glass of juice, Louis told Robert, "Go and may the damned go with you". Elizabeth and Michele had long thought it time for their celebration to conclude. So, with that and with a hardy "Good night to all"...and one last toast, the evening came to a close. The entire settlement could hear Louis on the way back to the trading post as he sang, with an uneducated French accent and a cracked, off key, voice most every French song he had ever known.

The sun rose on a quiet, warm and beautiful spring day. However, neither Robert nor Louis were in any condition to appreciate its beauty. They were both uttering only disjointed sounds and strangled groans. It was not until Elizabeth breathed a heavy, loud, exasperated sigh that Robert's feet finally hit the floor. Better than half the morning was gone and much needed to be done before the wagon train departed.

Somehow, during the next two weeks, ample supplies were stocked in the cabin along with as much wood for the fireplace that Robert could possible chop. He was doing everything possible to amend for his and Louis's actions during the "celebration". Additionally, he began to gather his medical supplies, his bedroll, rifle and all the other equipment he would require on his trip west.

He took time to locate and visit with the new doctor that had arrived. After a rather lengthy visit, he assured himself this new doctor was amply qualified. Word had traveled fast that Doctor Wood would be leaving with the next train and Robert wished to personally visit with as many of his patients as he could find to put their mind at ease. He assured them Doctor Samuel Spurgeon and his wife, Betsy, who had had nursing training, would be available and fully capable to handle their entire requirement.

The wagon train, with "Brother Black" as the wagon master, began to form down by the river crossing. They would cross the river yet today and would join the main body from Florence, Nebraska territory, which were already on the west bank awaiting their arrival. Everyone was anticipating the start of the exciting journey to the "Promised Land".

With much trepidation, Robert and Elizabeth said their good byes. He planted little kisses along her cheek. He bent his head and kissed her in the hollow of her throat. She wrapped both arms around him and crushed him to her. She felt a whisper of fear go through her and was not relieved much when she observed his face as it also betrayed a certain tension. This was their first parting since their marriage and it had happened with seemingly such suddenness.

With arms draped lightly around each other, they began the short walk to the wagon to which Robert had been assigned. He slapped her fondly on the buttocks, turned quickly, and climbed aboard the wagon. She tried to protest his leaving but her vocal chords stalled.

She, with their month old son, George Adelbert in her arms and Michele and Louis by her side, stood motionless until the wagon disappeared from sight.

Chapter 11

The Boundless Prairie……. Summer/Fall 1848

The wagon train of 300 wagons, with about 1800 souls, left that morning just after another group from the east bank arrived. A solemn "departing" religious celebration was held the night before the departure. "Brother" Jesse Black gave detailed instructions that had to be followed without question by all individuals on "His" Wagon Train. All of the instructions seemed like common sense to Robert for anyone going into the unknown.

As much as possible the wagon train was to follow the Oregon Trail that had recently been somewhat documented. They would be traveling about 1300 miles but there would be stops at the newly established forts along the way: Fort Kearney, Fort Laramie and Fort Bridger.

Since supplies would be limited, each wagon had been instructed to carry as many supplies as possible. The group had further been told of the many problems that they would encounter and that would have to be overcome. It would be up to each individual to share the work evenly, support one another, and make sure all survive this perilous journey.

For the first few days most walked, talked, and smiled greetings to each other on every possible occasion. This, however, grew burdensome as the wagon wheels churned out their endless clouds of dust that at times blurred even the horizon. Dust, dust and more dust choking the throats and nostrils of both human and the animal. Clouds of this yellow dust settled everywhere in the wagons, in their food and on the travelers themselves. While the evening bivouacs were a most welcome break from the infernal dust, they found the night dew and the dust made grime, which required additional attention for the wagons axles as well as in many other areas.

As time went on, if it was not the dust, it became the endless prairie grass, the rolling hills and ravines that slowed the progress. Occasionally they passed a small group of wagons returning to the east. They learned these folks had set out to seek their fortunes in the gold fields recently discovered at the end of the Oregon Trail. The traveling difficulties had become far too great for them to continue their journey. Their felt their "dreams" had been cruelly broken by the element. Some on the Mormon wagon train wished they could join them, but the doctrine of the Church, their faith, and the promise made by Brigham Young of a "new life", proved greater than their longing.

On the third week, the train's advance scouts spotted quite a number of Indians. They reportedly did not appear too friendly, causing the wagons to pause and form a circle against possible attack.

While the Indians approached the wagon train, close enough for their "War Paint" to be seen, they departed without incident. It was surmised and confirmed by "Brother" Black that the size of the wagon train and its preparedness had discouraged them. The Indians, however, continued for days to follow the uncomfortable travelers in the wagon train. Many other times during the next few months, Indians would be seen in the distance but nothing came of these sightings.

On the fifth week, the pioneers stopped by a small river for the night. It was shortly after dinner that a small puff of smoke was observed coming from a gully nearby.

All too quickly, the smoke rose to meet the horizon and the western sunset became blood red. Massive flames soon began to bathe the site where the wagon train was camped.

Flames spread though the dry prairie grasses and prairie chickens scurried from the hot updrafts. One of the worst disasters that all had been warned about was occurring before their very eyes. The fire, driven by a gentle breeze from the west, caught two of the wagons on the outer fringes of the camp. Only quick action in forming a bucket brigade from the nearby river that they had luckily camped by this night saved, perhaps, the entire wagon train from complete disaster.

It was shortly learned that two young boys, off on their own adventure, had accidentally started the fire as they successfully caught some of the last hot rays of the setting sun with their father's magnifying glass.

Doctor Wood was immediately caring for the burns the boys had suffered and those suffered by others who had been unceremoniously called on to fight the fire. As always, Robert rose to the occasion with relish and a firm command of the situation.

As the days turned into weeks and the weeks into months, there was always work for the weary doctor. Each day brought new and different problems and among them, the treating of snakebites was not uncommon.

One day he helped bury one of the young travelers beside a tree near the river. As the train was crossing a particular rough and rugged gully, she fell from her horse and landed on her head. He could not save her from the damage that had been caused. This part of doctoring was the most difficult for Robert.

Another day he treated the victim of an accidental gunshot. Although rather critical, Robert was successful in his operation, which was done during a noontime break and in place of eating. The victim remained under Robert's close care in the back of the wagon for the next week.

As promised, the train did stop for a few days at each of the army frontier forts: Fort Kearney, Fort Laramie, and Fort Bridger. While the rest of the wagon train was resting, Robert was visiting with the medical doctors at each fort in hopes of replenishing his supplies.

At Fort Bridger, he met a frontier doctor who had served years before with Dr. Muir, the same doctor who had influenced Robert's initial move to Hart's Bluff. They had a great deal to discuss and were sorry that their time together was cut short by "Brother" Black's brisk announcement: "Prepare! The train will continue in the morning next."

The next weeks were uneventful and gave a number of the elders cause to talk with renewed vigor to "convert" Robert. The good doctor continued to resist, and with the intense attention he started to receive became sure that Jesse Dunlap had instructed them to "work on Doc Wood" before they reached the "Promised Land". "Will they never stop?", Robert questioned in his mind.

The wagon train turned southwest as it left Fort Bridger. This was the trail that the Brigham Young expedition had established the year previously and was now commonly known as the Mormon Trail.

As it passed into Emigration Canyon, excitement began to erupt among the wagons. The long hard trip was almost over, with but fifty miles remaining, before they reached their destination. They stopped that night just outside the western end of the canyon. This permitted an exceptional evening view of the basin that spread out below them. They stood in enchanted surprise and with awe as they watched the magic of the evening sunset as it wove its colorful bright pattern across the sky and as the last rays of the sun played in a silvery glow on the waters of a great lake. This was everything they had expected of the "Promised Land". Even the moon that night seemed to be bent on hurrying them on their way as it bounced from one dark cloud to another.

The next day, the final day, was to start early to assure reaching their final goal before sundown. Early to bed was advised by "Brother" Black. Sleep finally nudged the thoughts of tomorrow from their minds.

The next day was spent in controlled excitement as the travelers pulled into the basin of the "Promised Land". This controlled excitement quickly turned to jubilation as the wagon train approached the last five miles and many from the settlement rode out to greet them.

However, it was not long before they discovered that a land filled with milk, honey and flowing fountains, as many had surmised, was not to be had.

Chapter 12

The Return Home......... August 1848

True to his word and "The Contract", Robert stayed another month after they arrived. During this time, he was called on many times to perform his "Magic" on many new patients. In his spare time, he acquainted himself with the various activities of the community.

He found the construction of the temple of particular interest. It had already been started and was to be the center of other church buildings, which were to be erected. He sat and watched the numerous ant-like men laboring to complete it as quickly as possible. His interest did not go unnoticed by some of the elders who previously had discussed their religion with him.

When it came time for him to leave for home, he was the recipient of a "send off" community party attended by the many friends he had made. While he welcomed the party and enjoyed the time with his friends, he felt "The Party" was little more than an excuse for an "evening tea get together" and was nothing like most other parties. Nonetheless, he said his sad good byes. He would leave the next morning in good spirit, with money in his pocket and a good horse beneath him.

Very early that August 15th morning, he rode out to meet Lot Smith and George Lake, the two mail couriers he was to accompany back east. They were both experienced with all the required trail and riding skills for which he had hoped.

Robert immediately felt comfortable with Lot. He was tall and straight with budging muscles that instilled the feeling of a safe journey home. George, on the other hand, was a red haired gangly youth with a blotchy face and an easy laugh, both of which did not speak well of him. Robert's feelings about George proved to be incorrect.

During the almost month long trip home, Robert learned a great deal about each of them, their lives, their parents and was truly saddened when it came time for parting. They had also grown fond of Robert and his interesting storytelling. They all pledged to meet up again.

Upon reaching Council Bluffs, Robert immediately rode up to the cabin on the hill without stopping to greet either Frank Ragland or Louis LaRoche as he passed their dwellings.

So as not to startle Elizabeth too greatly, he knocked on the door of the cabin and proclaimed loudly, "Mother, I'm home.", then paused briefly before opening the door.

Elizabeth turned to face the opening cabin door and froze in pleased surprise. Then, a cry louder than that of 7-month-old Adelbert in the corner of the cabin, rang from her mouth. The cabin erupted in the wonderful feeling of happiness.

Robert instantly noticed there had been a softening in Elizabeth during his absence that was like a magnetic pull on his masculinity. As Elizabeth kissed his tanned, weather beaten face, she became aware that he had gained a new rugged masculine appeal that she found disturbingly attractive.

So began their first night together in five long months. George Adelbert's periodic cries from his corner of the cabin went unanswered.

In the morning, Robert put his bedroll outside on the cabin roof to air. He then began to empty his saddle bags on the cabin floor. He was grinning from ear to ear as he handed Elizabeth dollar bill after dollar bill and coins of all description.

Never had she seen so much wealth at one time and in such an attractive pile. Like "moneygrubbers", they ran their fingers around, over and through this intoxicating pile of money that now reposed on the cabin floor. And, of course, he announced, he also now had a new sturdy horse, which was certainly worth a considerable sum.

They began to discuss what should be done with all this newfound wealth. Elizabeth's thoughts quickly turned to new items for Adelbert and various other items she needed for the cabin. Robert's thoughts were more about where to hide it so it would not be spent too quickly.

Before they left the breakfast table, it was decided that Robert would cut a small hole in the cabin floor and the money would be placed in this "secret" compartment. With Elizabeth's caution that rats might possibly destroy the cache, it was further decided it would first be placed inside a metal box in which Robert had kept some of his medicines.
So it was done, save a small amount that was needed for some new supplies now that Robert was back home.

With Adelbert in her arms and Robert by her side, they set off down the hill to see Louis and Michele. On their way, Robert became aware of the growth that had taken place in the settlement during the short time he had been away. More Mormons had arrived each day, he was told. However, most of their earlier Mormon friends had moved on to the "Promised Land".

Undoubtedly, Robert had passed them on his trip back home without knowing. He explained that since they had returned by horseback, they had taken many short cuts, which were many miles distant from the trail necessary for the wagon train. He felt sorry to have passed so closely without seeing and greeting them. They had all become such close friends over the few years that they had all shared the original Hart's Bluff.

Robert took the time to go and visit with all his remaining friends and earlier patients in the area, to let them know he had returned and to tell them of his adventure. In the next few weeks, his medical practice began to thrive. He took time to visit extensively with Dr. Contrell and his wife Sally, who confirmed the area could now easily support both doctors and their families in good fashion.

Robert's and Elizabeth's journey into the unknown had just been three years too early. The advice Dr. Muir had given Robert to "Go West" had been right and proper. Robert wrote a letter to Dr. Muir that very day to let him know how the area had grown and about his adventures with the Mormon wagon train.

Robert's patient list and his reputation built quickly as he continued to treat the Mormons as the various wagon trains passed through this part of the frontier.

Some enterprising families from the trains stopped to spend a year or two or their lifetime in the fertile farm land and valleys around Council Bluffs. Also, with the increased traffic to and from Council Bluffs, the entire area became widely known and recognized for the bountiful harvests that could be produced. Others hearing this were attracted and came to the area.

Many were of German heritage, who found the land similar to that they had left in the "Old Country", far more fertile and without the persecution by the government that had been so common.

Freedom was present on this new frontier for all who truly relished it and were capable of handling the difficulties and harshness it always offered.

Chapter 13

Duty Calling.........
Late 1848 to April 1850

The winter of 1848 was unusually mild which gave the growing population a season without hard labor and pleasant weather to visit and become even a closer knit community.

Elizabeth and Robert's second son, David, was born May 1849 and Elizabeth became pregnant again in the early fall.

Doc Wood continues to be the physician of choice with the Mormons in the various settlements, now along both sides of the Missouri river. He was also the choice of the wagon trains in their ever-increasing numbers as they passed through the area throughout the summer and fall of 1849.

In early spring of 1850, a special rider going east stopped at Robert and Elizabeth's cabin. As Robert opened the cabin door, he quickly recognized George Lake. Still a courier, and still with red hair and easy laugh, but gone was his gangly youth and the blotchy face that had been his trademark when Robert had ridden with him two years previously. He now possessed a body that had evolved into one of strength, power and muscular endurance.

Robert was pleased to see him and Elizabeth was taken by the poise and strength exerted by this young man of which she had heard so much. In their early greetings, Robert asked about Lot Smith and learned he had married and was now living in an area far to the southwest named St. George which had recently been established by the church They had a lot more reminiscing to do before they got down to the reason for the visit.

The real reason was to personally deliver a number of letters from Prophet Brigham Young and from other Elders and friends Doctor Wood had treated in the past. Prior to leaving, George Lake mentioned to Robert that he had been charged, in a personal audience with Prophet Young, that he was to receive the assurance from Robert that a reply would be made promptly. Robert assured him he would read the letters and do so promptly. Knowing Robert's word was good, George bid his goodbyes, was out the door, on his horse and on his way without looking back.

The letters told Robert of a mysterious sickness that was spreading throughout the new settlement and pleaded with him to come quickly. He was elated with the confidence their request showed in him.

The yet unborn baby presented a dilemma, and he recalled a few years previous a similar situation that had kept him home. He toiled with a hurried decision, but it was not long before the epidemic situation along with the Oath he had taken upon becoming a physician, won out, truly giving him no other choice.

Rather than sending a reply to Brigham Young, knowing he could get there himself just as fast as a letter, he left with the next mail couriers moving west. He expected to return before the baby was born, but just in case, he made arrangements with Doctor Contrell and his wife, Sally, to handle the birth. Subsequently, Lou Wood was born in April 1950 without Robert present, having left two months before.

By sheer luck, he caught the returning trip to what was now known as "Salt Lake" with his young friend, George Lake.

Both welcomed another journey together and Prophet Young would surely be pleased with George's quick action and his ability to have "persuaded" Robert to make such a dedicated response to the request for help.

During the long days on the trail, Robert had time to consider what this mysterious sickness might be. From how it had been described in the various letters he had received, it sounded strangely like Cholera. While living in Chicago, shortly after graduation from Physicians College, Robert had experienced Cholera first hand. However, Cholera was usually the result of unsanitary conditions and he knew the Mormons were generally very fastidious in their hygiene. Robert's mind turned to various other diseases as frequently as the turns in the trail. Whatever it was, he felt confident the problem could be solved in time.

As George and Robert arrived at their destination, Robert first noticed the completed church and its towers appearing as outstretched arms, seemingly reaching to the heavens. "Very impressive and fast work", Robert thought. Its construction had just begun to take shape when he left the area just two years previously.

Their pending arrival had been announced to Prophet Brigham Young by one of the outlining scouts who had spotted their approach and reported it the day before. Both were immediately given an audience with Prophet Young who didn't hide his sparkle of pleasure upon seeing Doctor Wood standing before him once again and obviously ready to "serve".

They got right down to the business at hand. The problem had gotten worse since the letters had been written and it appeared to be becoming a full blown epidemic throughout the young settlement. Brigham Young pleaded with Robert to act as quickly as possible.

With that, and the names and location of some of the more serious cases, Robert departed to begin his investigation without pausing to locate a place to stay that night.

His first stop was at the home of Howard Egan and his wife Helen. Helen was the more sick of the two. Howard described her symptoms as follows and Robert began writing in his book after Helen Egan's name, as each was mentioned.....

> Diarrhea,
> Gas,
> Stomach cramps,
> Nausea,
> and dehydration...... all of which had been going on for 3 weeks, at least.

When Robert examined Helen, he found her to be a real fright. Howard had most of the same problems but nowhere nearly as bad as Helen. Quickly, Robert pressed him for possible reasons for this difference.

It was not until Robert was preparing to leave that Howard, recognizing Robert's fatigue, offered him a small libation. Such an offer was almost unheard of by any true practicing Mormon and Robert was surprised and somewhat taken back by the offer but did not hesitate to accept the invitation.

As they sat together sipping their drinks, Robert realized, almost as if hit by a bolt of lightening, that that was the reason why Howard had not been affected as had been his wife Helen. He began making notes in his book. The alcohol, of course, helped control the spread of whatever germs were entering the bodies' system.

This was confirmed after further questioning; Howard sheepishly admitted that he frequently took a little nip almost every day when he got home. But in so admitting, asked Robert to treat his confession with confidence for the sake of peace and harmony amongst their many Mormon friends. With a second little nip, Robert agreed to do so.

For Helen, Doc Wood prescribed one spoonful of salt; one of sugar mixed in $1/8^{th}$ of a glass of apple vinegar and filed with water. Helen was to sip this slowly, and when this full glass was gone, to start on another glass of the same and continue this procedure, as often as possible, until he returned tomorrow morning.

Howard started to pay Doc Wood but was waved off. But Howard would have none of that and, at the very least, offered the good doctor a bed for the night. Robert quickly accepted but told him he must make a few more calls yet that night. He would return as soon as possible and hopefully share one nighttime nip with Howard before bedding down for the much needed sleep he felt coming on.

After four quite similar home visits, he returned as promised, unsaddled his horse and turned in for the night between two clean luxurious sheets.

Chapter 14

The Investigation ....

Howard was exuberant the next morning when Robert joined him in the kitchen. Helen was already feeling quite a bit better. Robert quickly turned to investigate for himself. It was as Howard spoke. She was better and told Robert in a weak, rattled voice, that she was on her seventh glass of his awful prescribed concoction. Robert, while not showing it, was both pleased and surprised it had produced results so quickly.

As he made his rounds to the other homes he had visited the night before, he found the same was true. The patients were all somewhat better. And all thanked Robert profusely. He made another twenty or more home visits before stopping for the day and returning to the same clean luxurious sheets he had become acquainted with the night before. He sat with Howard and wondered aloud what the cause for this outbreak could possible be. Robert quizzed Howard on subject, after subject, in his attempt to uncover the source of this mystery. He realized that in the discovery lay the total solution to the sickness. Time was important.

On each home visit he made, he paused after treating the patient to question more closely all present and in depth. When had it started? What was changed or was different than before? He gathered this information and little by little recorded it in his notebook for further consideration at a later time.

Slowly, an inkling of some clues began to emerge. He had recorded that many families had visited the Great Salt Lake for a swim.

While this did not seem unusual in the least, what was surprising was that many of them also mentioned the unusual birds that dove into the water to catch fish. Always the inquisitive, Robert had to go see this for himself.

After lunch on the sixth day after his arrival, Howard and Robert set off to travel the few miles to the area on the lake that this bird novelty had been observed. Sure enough, the area was alive with lots of birds doing exactly that, which had been described, diving into the waters to catch fish for dinner. As Robert watched in fascination of the acrobatics of these creatures, his mind was churning, wondering what, if any, connection there could be between what he was seeing and the illness itself.

He returned the next day after first visiting the small Mormon library of books that had been brought across the prairie with the very first wagon train. The Library had very few books but he found a book he felt might help. He asked to borrow the book for a day or so, much to the surprise of the ladies in charge. They obviously wondered why the good doctor took time from his patients to go bird watching. Ignoring their quizzical looks, he rode off toward the lake with the book in his saddlebag. Sitting on the beach, he watched the diving birds for sometime before reaching for the book he had brought. Just as he had done with each of his patients, he wrote in his little book a description of the birds he observed.

*Length about 9 inches, wingspan perhaps 22-24 ".

*Stocky-bodied with short, thin bill with lower mandible beveled upwards at the tip.

*Black bill with pale tip feet set far back on body and tail awkwardly behind body in flight.

*Head triangular with peak towards center of the head, slate
    grey head with whitish flanks and belly.

He easily found the bird in the book he had brought. It was
an Eared Grebes. He further learned that the birds were well
known around the Great Lake region, especially near
Chicago. While he did not recall having seen the birds when
he was living in Chicago, he did remember being told of
great flocks of birds passing the area each year as they
migrated south for the winter. Further study of the book
confirmed these facts.

Each night after returning home, he would study the notes he
had made over the past days, seeking both the cause and
source of this Avian Cholera.

He was beginning to feel like a character in one of the
mystery books he enjoyed. He had many clues but no
solution. In the three weeks he had been there, he had treated
over two hundred patients that had been affected by this
mystery disease.

The clues obtained so far were as follows:

*Individuals who had swum in the Great Salt Lake had
    become ill.
*Large flocks of diving birds had been observed by most,
    if not all, the swimmers.
*Others who had not visited the lake had also come down
    with the illness.

What caused it in them was not known but possibly had been
from something they had drunk. Water was the only
common element.

But the houses of the ill individuals were spread throughout the entire community and the number of new reported cases had not slowed. Some patients had died of dehydration. In addition, from the looks of things many more would soon be going.

Robert decided to further follow the drinking water clue and at the break of day was off to revisit those patients who had this as a possible common element. By noon, he had another clue. No wells had yet been dug by these families but rather they depended on the water service supplier who delivered fresh water to them in large wooden barrels every few days, depending on their individual requirements.

After lunch, Robert set off to visit with the supplier of this fresh water. He had been directed to follow the small stream near the east trail entrance to the settlement that flowed from the foothills. The river was easily found but Robert was surprised to find it only a very small flowing trickle, hardly enough to be called a river. Nonetheless, he began following it eastward into the foothills that surrounded the settlement on that side.

He stopped at the first cabin he came to seeking further direction. He learned that he was going in the correct direction but still had about 5 miles to go to reach the cabin of William Allen, the provider of fresh water. Without Robert asking, they also volunteered the fact that the river had slowed its flow considerably since last fall and had been wondering why it had happened. Robert recorded this information in his book as he had done so many times before, then continued on his way.

It was not long before he reached the cabin of William Allen and was told that William was further upriver filling barrels at this very moment. It was about three o'clock in the afternoon when Robert finally came upon William at work, filling the barrels.

William had contrived a hoist system for lifting the empty barrels from his buck board into a small dam to fill them and then return the heavier barrel back to the wagon. "Ingenious!" thought Robert. However, Robert immediately noticed the construction of the dam itself. It had originally been made by filling the river bed with rock and logs. Then debris washing out of the foothills had filled the cracks, creating a solid barrier to hold back the river water, thus forming a small pond.

Careful inspection showed that some of the material that had washed down was carcasses of birds and these appeared to be carcasses of Eared Grebes.

Talking to William Allen, he asked him outright about the birds. William told him, yes, many had just washed down, but these feathered creatures seemed to fill the leaks in the dam so efficiently he had brought a few wagonloads down from an area in the mountains and had physically, strategically, placed them amongst the timbers and the rocks as packing. Robert concluded quickly, "Obviously, these were carcasses of infected diving Grebes".

To further investigate, Robert rode on up the river with William to the place he said he had earlier gathered the birds. In spite of the fact William had taken many away, there remained thousands more in various states of decay.

Apparently, this sheltered valley had been the nesting spot to which the flocks returned after their feeding at the lake. They had left sick, returned to this secluded site and died, perhaps partly due to the extra exertion of the round trip flight. This would seem to explain the vast quantity of dead birds in this one location. This also meant that some of the birds had died on the flight over to the lake or actually in the lake itself.

As Robert wrote feverishly in his book, he began to softly smile to himself. "That was it", he thought.

The patients who had visited the lake to swim had contracted the illness from the contaminated water or from the droppings from the contaminated birds that had flown over the beaches. And the others were infected by the delivered drinking water. Without finishing his writing or his final conclusions, he thanked William, told him to deliver no more drinking water to the settlement until he got back to him and road off in a hurry toward the settlement and hopefully an early audience with Brigham Young.

He had no delay in obtaining an audience. It was set for the next day at mid-morning at the church headquarters. It just happened that his request for an audience had come at the same time as the church's normally scheduled monthly Elder's meeting. Elders from across the entire settlement would be present to discuss various church issues of which this was certainly one. Robert worked into the late night in preparation for this meeting. He wanted to be thorough in his explanation of his discovery and ready to answer any question that may be presented.

Chapter 15

Presenting the Solution........

He reviewed all the notes he had made to assure his conclusions were all proper. He then set out to list the elements necessary to correct the problem.

1. Ban all swimming and picnicking at the Great Lake until at least the next hard freeze. Then patrol the beaches, lake, and rivers for any possible new signs of the birds that had brought this Avian Cholera. Be aware that heavy winds sweeping across the Great Lake from the north, would deposit dead birds with Cholera on the south shore. Act accordingly.

2. Do not pick up or personally handle these birds in any way. Watch your pets for signs of them having eaten, or otherwise contacted, an infected bird or even another animal.

3. Organize a clean up detail for the nesting grounds that had been discovered. All bird carcasses would have to be buried to assure other predatory animals would not carry them off. A new streambed and dam would have to be created which would supply fresh water for William Allen's water supplying business. Or new settlement deep wells provided for the community's daily water needs. The longer term solution was for a new dam to be built and properly policed and patrolled. Additionally, a new source of water must be obtained for the community. One from streams higher into the mountains may be the answer but would not necessarily assure against future contamination.

Protected, deep, producing wells situated throughout the settlement would seem to be the best immediate solution, and judging from the short time it had taken to build the new temple, that such an undertaking would not be a difficult task for the young community.

4. Gather the dead birds from the south beaches of the lake and likewise bury them in remotely located deep graves.

5. Inform all in the community of the discovered source of the problem and advise all to boil all water prior to its use. Even wash water, since the infection could be transferred by touching infected clothing and then touching ones hands to their mouths. Constant alertness will be required by all citizens of the settlement.

6. Be aware of any early onset of infection and treat it accordingly.

7. Advise all infected individuals to treat themselves with the special concoction of salt, sugar and vinegar in vast quantities of fresh clean water, thus preventing dehydration and possible death of the victim.

8. Be wise, be alert, be safe should be the motto during any mysterious illness or epidemic. Always be cautious of what one eats or drinks in every unproven frontier situation. Harkin back to the safety requirements established for the wagon trains as they had earlier set off across the untamed wilderness. Be ever vigilant.

9. Lastly, set up a special educational series for the settlement entitled: "Looking forward from the past". It would deal with the everyday risks of frontier life. Learning to anticipate and organize for new and unusual problems that the young community may encounter in the future.

Robert arrived early the next morning for his meeting and was greeted by both Elders Black and Jesse Dunlap who he had not seen since Winter Quarter a few years before. They were delighted to see Robert and anxious to learn of his conclusions on the mysterious illness. They did not have long to wait. Robert was to be the very first speaker at this important meeting.

As he stood and walked to the front of the room, he received short greetings as he passed various elders with whom he had become acquainted. These softly spoken greetings had made him feel comfortable as he began his recount of that which he had learned.

He first announced the cause of the mystery illness and provided the name to the council … "Cholera"! After the surprise gasps from the audience died down, Robert continued with an explanation. "A person may get cholera by drinking water or eating food contaminated with the cholera bacterium. In an epidemic, the source of the contamination is usually the feces of an infected person or that of various birds or animals. The disease can spread rapidly in areas with inadequate treatment of sewage and drinking water". "The cholera bacterium may also live in the environment in rivers and coastal waters, including lakes. Fish eaten raw have been a source of cholera. The disease is not likely to spread directly from one person to another; therefore, casual contact with an infected person is not a risk for becoming ill. As far as food and drink, a simple rule of thumb is...... Boil it, cook it, peel it, or forget it. Eat only foods that have been thoroughly cooked and are still hot, or fruit that you have peeled yourself."

The entire audience was very attentive and became even more so as Robert began to discuss the various points in the solution he had prepared the night before.

On the conclusion of his speech, the prophet Brigham Young himself spoke first and thanked him for his quick action to the problem. He further assured Robert that each of his points would be acted upon during the remaining days of this important council gathering and done so without undue delay.

As the session broke for lunch, Robert overheard many of the Elders in conversation discussing the solutions he had presented. One of the comments he overheard was that Brigham Young was much taken with the idea of including "Looking forward from the past" in all frontier education throughout the settlements.

Another comment overheard was that they recognized the sacrifice Robert had made by leaving his pregnant wife to come help them in their time of true need, that that surely meant that Doc Wood must be one of them in his deep down beliefs since that is exactly what any good Mormon would do for the benefit of the group. As he heard this, Robert merely smiled inwardly to himself.

For the next two weeks, he continued to make house calls on patients. He had now been to over 600 families' homes since his arrival and was becoming very well known throughout the settlement.

Of course, the money he had been given for his service was also very welcome, but he was beginning to long for home. In fact, he had started to prepare for his return to Council Bluffs when he received a special summons from Brigham Young.

As Robert had previously overheard, Brigham Young now told him personally that he was much taken with his dedication to duty over family and hoped to persuade him to spend a little longer time before leaving. He explained to Robert that he wanted him to establish the nucleus of the special educational studies program that he had suggested at the earlier Elders meeting.

With Robert's medical background, his experience with frontier life, and his obvious friendliness and common sense, he was the natural choice for this undertaking in various other new settlements. Such settlements had been commissioned by the Church and were springing up throughout this new frontier area that now stretched as far as the eye could see and beyond.

Brigham Young then surprised Robert with a reward for his services and for his solution to the mystery illness. The reward was beyond Robert's wildest dreams. One thousand dollars had been voted by the Elders, in gratitude for Robert's service and was now given to him, along with a handshake and a hearty pat on the back by the head of this Church group.

Then, without hesitation, Brigham offered Robert a new contract, one that could not be refused, along with his promise of his personal support in helping Robert establish the special educational groups obviously so dearly needed across this new frontier.

Robert was assured that whatever was needed to accomplish such a task, he would receive, and as for Elizabeth, back in Council Bluffs, she would be safety transported to this new frontier should that be Robert's request, or he could just send her money with the couriers as had previously been discussed.

As Robert sat quietly to ponder the offer, Brigham handed him a letter, which had come the day before from Elizabeth. It informed him everything was fine with her and the boys. The third child, another boy, had been born just two weeks after he had left. She had named the baby Lou, as they had agreed. Both she and the baby were doing just fine.

An Indian girl named Wapeka, of the Pottawanamee tribe across the river, who was also a acquaintance of Choovio, the young girl who had became the wife to Frank Ragland, was now staying at the cabin and helping with the chores of raising the two older boys as well as helping to care for the new baby.

Elizabeth reported things were quite easy for her and she truly liked the freedom that the help from Wapeka permitted. The name meant Skillful, so Louis La Rouche had told her, and she certainly was living up to her name. Of course, Elizabeth continued, she must pay the young girl for her services and that the money set aside in the hole in the floor was disappearing with each week. Could he send more with the courier?

He certainly could and did so with the next courier leaving for Council Bluffs. Robert now had more than money and prestige that he had ever thought possible and he felt comfortable and at home with these people that he once had thought "Strange" and distant.

With his mind at ease about Elizabeth, he reasoned he could take a few more months in the area, do the biddings of the Church, and serve the kind, generous people in the outlying areas. In fact, he secretly relished the idea of the further adventure and the exploring he was being offered in this new land of wonders. He rationalized: this would also make it possible for Elizabeth to keep her Indian girl helper indefinitely.

A sixth month "Contract" was made and signed the next day by Brigham Young himself, and by Jesse Dunlap as a witness. This would mean Robert would be staying through the winter months and depart for home in the early spring. However, this was not to be.

Chapter 16

The Contract Extension ....
Fall 1850 / Winter 1853

Many new needs arose throughout the new Utah territory as the Mormons expanded rapidly in all directions leading in and away from Salt Lake City, especially to the south and southwest.

Robert traveled to the most distant settlements, establishing his educational programs during the early winter months prior to the heavy snows. Everyone seemed to know about his six months contract and great pressure was put on Doc Wood in every community he visited to remain even after the six months contract was to expire.

He continued to resist these many calls and invitations to join the Church of Jesus Christ of Latter Day Saints. He received ever increasing innuendoes and lectures on Mormonism throughout the entire winter and especially so from Elder William C. Allen with whom he spent the heavy snowy winter months in the St. George area, a settlement in a fertile valley about 200 miles to the southwest of the main Salt Lake Settlement.

With the early spring, Prophet Brigham Young arrived for a short vacation stay at his summer cabin in the mountains to the west. One of the first things he did was to seek out Dr. Wood to discuss how the educational program was proceeding and to discover how his medical practice was progressing.

He used this discussion to also try to convince him to stay a little longer, or at least until other doctors arrived who could handle the ever increasing health problems brought on by the fast population increase. Long into one night, the two discussed various issues facing the new communities throughout the entire Utah settlement.

Such issues included the following on which Robert took notes:

Health....Personal hygiene education to some form of regional hospitals.

Water systems and supplies.....Including individual households and larger scale irrigation systems.

Sanitation...The production and disposal of wastes.

Social Welfare.... Assurance to all settlers of food, shelter and health necessities.

Safety and Security needs.

After their discussions ended about midnight, Robert spent the night in a room that had been prepared for him by Prophet Young's wives. He lit a candle and sat on the edge of his bed as he studied his notes of the meeting. His head was swimming with various thoughts concerning the discussion. Many of them seemed to lead to new opportunities for him personally. He scribbled notes to himself and did not fall asleep until almost daybreak.

After breakfast, Robert spoke again to Brigham Young, pointing out various other opportunities he saw to further help throughout the settlements.

Brigham Young listened intently as Robert outlined his plan to expand his current visitations to the various settlements by incorporating education and direction in the accomplishment of at least the first three points of the previous night's discussion. Further, through the contacts on his visits, he would be in a prime position to report back on and hopefully advance the solutions on the two remaining points. Robert explained he felt the latter two points could be achieved with little extra effort.

And so began Dr. Wood's extended contract with the Mormon Church. To Robert, this meant more money to send home by courier to Elizabeth and the three boys, still in Council Bluffs, Iowa Territory. To the Prophet it meant the Church would have the good doctor a bit longer to do the Church's work throughout the territory and, with this extra time, certainly they could win him over and make him a full fledged member of the Church of Jesus Christ of Latter Day Saints.

Robert's letter to Elizabeth, sent the next day, explained the new contract, and that with the extra money he was enclosing, which he had received as a special bonus, she and the boys would be far better taken care of than if he was to return at this time and struggle to restart his practice in Council Bluffs.

He explained he had been offered additional responsibilities, resulting in increased travel throughout this new and fascinating land, and as long as he knew she and the family were well provided for, he felt she would understand and appreciate the destiny, which finally seemed to be coming their way.

Robert continued his efforts throughout all the settlements. He spent a week or so in each of these settlements, staying with an Elder of the Church who had previously been contacted by Prophet Young and instructed to handle all the needs of Dr. Wood.

Leaving St. George, Robert traveled north in the next few months to Pinto Creek, then on to Harmony, Cedar City, Parowan, Beaver, Corn Creek and to Fillmore where he turned west to Sevier Lake.

He had heard of a United States survey expedition headed by Captain John Gunnison in the area that was exploring a route for a railroad to the Pacific Ocean. Robert wished to see and visit with the Captain whom he had briefly known as a Lieutenant years before in Council Bluffs, and further obtain news of home and beyond.

From Fillmore's village President, Anson Call, Robert learned that local Indian conditions in the Sevier Lake area were somewhat unsettling, even dangerous. He further learned that several nearby bands of Pah Vantes, led by Chief Kanosh, had recently had a tragic encounter with a party of emigrants bound for California, and the chief's son had been injured in the attack. Robert previously had preformed his medicine on numerous members of the tribe, knew the Chief well, and felt compelled to again offer his help. Although noting possible danger, Robert had an unusual feeling of security because of his past relationships with the various tribes.

Robert located the survey party with the help of various Indians he met along the way. He caught up with the Captain and his detail of twenty two men at the village of Manti in mid October 1853.

As Robert and Captain Gunnison sat near the campfire for warmth, they reminisced and the Captain brought Robert up to date about the rapid growth of Council Bluffs. This was being brought on by the migration of Mormon travelers from as far away as Denmark and England. Council Bluffs had become the natural stopping place for final preparation of the long and dangerous journey to the Promised Land. Robert was told that his oldest son was helping at Frank Ragland's stable and the last he saw of him; even at his young age was learning something of blacksmithing. This verbalized personal glimpse gave Robert some reassuring feelings, yet strong longings for home.

As dusk began to turn to darkness, Captain Gunnison and Robert's discussion turned to the job at hand. Robert gave the Captain the message he had been carrying from President Call of Fillmore. It assured the survey detail that peace had been made with this particular band of Indians and a guarantee had been reached so the survey detail could proceed safely with their work.

The next morning Robert departed for the tribe's location to administer whatever aid he might to the chief's son. Upon arrival, he discovered there had been no attack, no injuries, and no immigrant involvement as he had been told in Fillmore. Chief Kanosh said all these stories had been spoken with "forked tongue" and that the Pah Vantes were seeking no vengeance on anyone.

Seven days later Robert traveled to the settlement of Nephi were he learned that the Gunnison survey had been brutally attacked and all were killed, save four, who had survived to report the massacre. It had happened two days after Robert had visited with Captain Gunnison.

Gunnison had split his attachment into two groups, each with a particular assignment, in hopes of completing their work before the first snow. One of the groups, the one Gunnison himself commanded, had become the victims of an Indian attack. A group of possibly thirty Indians had surrounded his camp during the night, and at dawn, they attacked the survey crew and soldiers with rifle fire and arrows. Then they plundered the camp and butchered their victims.

Robert learned later that the rescue efforts by the other soldier detachment a day or two after the massacre had produced no survivors and had discovered the Gunnison campsite at about dusk. Rather than risk ambush themselves, the rescue team of soldiers "stood to horse" through the night while listening to the wolves devour their comrades. The next morning they buried the remains of their fallen   comrades. Captain Gunnison's body was deliberately left unburied. There had been a quarrel amongst the remaining officers and blame was placed on Gunnison for splitting his command, which resulted in the massacre.

Even later, Robert learned in confidence that a particular Indian tribe had been induced by the higher authority of the Church to do the deed in an effort to stop the possibility of a railroad through the area, and that the wealth obtained from their actions would be all theirs and no punishment would follow.

Robert knew that Chief Kanoch would not have been party to such deeds and that this attack had been carried off by one of the lesser tribes in the area. As far as Robert was concerned, Chief Kanoch was always good to his word. Robert knew Chief Kanoch would now be incensed by the thoughts that his tribe would be blamed by the Church for this deed.

Robert continued northward, stopping for a week or so at the settlements of Payson, Spanish Fork, Springville, Provo and Lehi. In each, he pursued his duties under the new contract and continued those under the older one to care for the sick and ailing as necessary.

As he arrived in Salt Lake City, he was astonished to observe the growth since his last visit to the area a few years previously.

The growth had been the result of Brigham Young's extensive programs to occupy all open territory in his control and to gain influence in the American nation. He had organized and began the Deseret Express and Carry Company to establish freight and mail relay stations from Missouri to San Francisco. He devised the inexpensive handcart method of bringing thousands of converts from Europe to Western America to establish villages along the emigration route to populate additional territories in the American Union. He had also undertaken a comprehensive religious reformation to purify his people so they could exercise the power of God to aid in the completion of their divine mission.

All of this became quickly apparent to Robert. There was much dissention amongst Robert's old friends concerning many of these actions, particularly when the handcart expedition proved so disastrous. Over one hundred and forty souls had perished on one such caravan, having been victims of an early winter snowstorm as they crossed the perilous desert on their way to the "Promised Land".

Robert's winter months were spent in review and in the refining of his educational programs in preparation for next spring. In addition to his growing medical practice, time was frequently spent with Brigham Young.

This time with the Prophet energized Robert and brought about a closer understanding and relationship. As Robert was to learn later, this was all a façade and part of Young's further plans to convert him to the Church's beliefs.

Chapter 17

A Break from Monotony....Summer 1854

As spring approached, renewed and increasing efforts were made by most everyone Robert knew in the Mormon Church to "win" Doc Wood over. On one meeting with Brigham Young in early spring, Robert was offered, in a commanding manner, a special trip to participate in a medical meeting in San Francisco. He was to travel with a group of Elders of the Church, with stops at various Mormon settlements along the way, and to visit the new Mormon Church that had recently been built in San Francisco.

For a welcome break in his work, as well as for the adventure of a trip further west, he gratefully accepted. He was told this break would not affect the agreement under which he had been contracted and to look at it as a reward of sorts, for his past efforts in his support of the Church's endeavors and expansion.

The trip was a true adventure, as Robert had hoped. The group of Elders, headed by Robert's old friend Elder Black, took the Hastings Cutoff route from Salt Lake to meet up with the California Trail. This trail had been followed by many travelers before and was much more established than the one Robert had first traveled west years earlier, with Elizabeth to Hart's Bluff.

As the group of travelers joined the California trail about midway to San Francisco, they were astonished to see the number of wagon trains that were on the trail. In speaking with the people on these trains, they learned that some had started in Independence, others in St. Joseph, and still others in Council Bluffs. At the mention of Council Bluffs, Robert's heart turned to Elizabeth and his boys. He realized letters from home had slowed, and in her last letter, she had mentioned that money was growing short. Robert had a difficult time understanding this since he had been sending large amounts of money home frequently with the Mormon courier. He had written Elizabeth a special letter of inquiry just before he had left Salt Lake City on this trip to San Francisco, and hoped to have her reply upon his return.

They took the Carson Route into Sacramento because it was shorter than the Truckee Route normally traveled, and they were traveling much lighter than the wagon trains they frequently passed. A few days later, they arrived in San Francisco and Robert had his first view of the massive blue Pacific Ocean and could hardly wait to get his feet into the water. He found time to do so the first night after their arrival at their hotel. A true city of luxury..... the likes of which Robert had not experienced since his time at school in Chicago.

The medical meeting was of major interest to Robert as he updated his knowledge and shared his experiences with others in his chosen profession. As a participant at this meeting, he had his picture taken by the official photographer and sent it off along with a letter by courier to Elizabeth the very next day.

Robert was particularly taken with the sailing ships in the harbor and spent much free time on the docks, watching arriving travelers as they too set off on new adventures in this wondrous new land of the West. He learned that some were heading to the gold fields to the south while others would be heading east to Salt Lake City, having traveled completely around the bottom of South America, all the way from Europe to reach the "Promised Land" they had heard about.

Each evening as Robert returned to the elegance of the hotel, the Elders would question him concerning his day. It was obvious to Robert that the pressure was still on for him to join the Mormon Church, bring his family to the area, build his medical practice with them rather than returning to Council Bluffs, and continue his work helping the Church.

Word got back to Robert through Elder Black, his old friend, that the other Elders had deemed him "Most stubborn, even incorrigible when it came to discussions on their religious beliefs". The truth of the matter, Robert admitted to his old friend, Elder Black, was that he was beginning to get exasperated by all the talk and pressure on the subject that had come his way since they had all left Salt Lake City on this trip.

That night, Robert lay in bed rethinking his conversation with Elder Black, and he became acutely aware of how different his beliefs were from the devoted Mormons with whom he had been living and had become accustomed. They somehow seemed vastly different from the "normal" people with whom he had come in contact in San Francisco.

Consequently, on the travel back home all conversation on the subject seemed to stop. Robert felt sure a report to Brigham Young on his comments, even given to his close friend in confidence, would be included. The Prophet would then know that the trip had really worked in reverse than that which had been expected.

Two days after their return to Salt Lake City, Robert received a message from Brigham Young that he was immediately to return to southwestern Utah since his services were most needed in that area.

On his trip south he had private time to think. Various conversations with old friends along the way caused him to grow increasingly skeptical of the actions, morality and intentions of the Mormons in general.

Upon his arrival at Christopher Baker's home, with whom he had stayed previously, he soon developed a peculiar feeling that he was being watched by most of the areas settlers, more closely than at any time previously. Conversations seemed to stop as he approached groups of his old friends.

It was his young courier friend, George Lake, from their earlier trip back home, that told him word had come down from Salt Lake to carefully watch Doc Wood because they didn't don't want this "prize" doctor to get away. George Lake also confided in Robert that all his mail, both incoming and outgoing, was being "monitored" by the Church. It was then Robert understood why he had received no letters from Elizabeth, and also why in the last one received, she had mentioned money was getting short.

Shocking, as it seemed, it was now apparent that money and the letters he had been sending home over the past six or eight months had not reached their destination. They had been intercepted, the money removed, and probably all destroyed for some strange reason known only to the Church itself ….the controller of all courier services.

Robert made up his mind: it was time to return to Council Bluffs before the next winter set in. But fate was to intervene and his return home, just yet, was not to be.

Chapter 18

The Obvious Prisoner 1854-55

The days passed slowly for Dr. Wood, with a procession like monotony.

With the lucrative contract now expired and the need to survive until he could escape this area of growing madness, his brow furrowed as he had the unusual sense of everything going wrong.

After an agony of indecision and in an effort to protect himself from physical harm, even death, which he knew had been bestowed on other non believers who had lost favor, he reluctantly vowed to change his attitude and outwardly, only outwardly, become what was necessary....a "Mormon of convenience".

He wondered if an outward charge of accepting the Church would be noticed, even welcomed, and if the change would be of any help to him at this late date as he continued to walk the knife-edge of danger.

He had become an unwilling prisoner of the area. To protect himself, and hopefully renew communications with Elizabeth, he must, out of necessity, change his attitude and outwardly become what he inwardly referred to as a "Mormon of convenience".

He concluded he must start rebuilding and expanding his medical practice in all the Mormon communities within the restricted day's ride that had been placed upon him. He also decided to extend his services, on a regular basis, to all of the nearby, friendly Indian villages who might welcome his "medicine". He remembered from his experiences in Hart's Bluff that Indians were more appreciative and always paid upon receipt of services. He liked, even needed, that arrangement at this time.

He wondered with being a "Mormon of convenience", not one of conviction; if he could indeed truly carry it off convincingly. He recognized only time would tell!!!!

A small but important shift in the Mormons' attitude toward him began to improve somewhat after Doc Wood was urgently summoned to Brigham Young's home to treat him for a very high fever.

The summer mountain retreat of Brigham Young was in the mountains, just a bit northwest of the St. George settlement, and to escape the heat of the desert and for recuperation, Prophet Young would visit the area as often as possible. On one such visit to the area, he had become frightfully ill and Doc Wood was the only physician immediately available. This would be the first time Robert had seen Young since before he had left for San Francisco and he approached it somewhat apprehensively.

Robert's examination determined that Brigham Young was suffering from an extreme case of "Mountain Sickness" brought on by mountain ticks. Brigham Young had experienced the same problems on his very first entry into the "Promised Land".

This time it was Robert who advised what the exact cause was of the sickness and how to prevent reoccurrences. One must inspect ones body after all visits into heavily wooded mountainous areas and carefully remove any offending ticks found before they could cause further problems, even death in some cases. Young's wives were very appreciative of Doc Wood's fast action in perhaps saving the Prophet's life. Word of his fete rapidly traveled throughout the area.

On one follow-up visit with his patient, Robert felt his presence was a bit undesired, especially by Brigham Young himself. The idea germinated that his once supportive and friendly patient had definitely changed and had no time for discussion with him on any subject as before. He felt Brigham Young was now carefully estimating him in every detail and seemingly setting a value. The thought whipped in so quickly that he had little time to consider what came next.

As Robert was leaving, no payment was offered, as was customary on all previous professional visits with the Prophet. On his ride back home, he searched anxiously for the full meaning behind the total change in attitude and the lack of payment. Two unsettling thoughts were that he had outlived his usefulness, even to the great man himself, or the Prophet had determined that Robert was merely a "Mormon of convenience", not one of conviction.

Before he was even halfway home, he made the commitment for further self-examination and reflection on his actions, his performance and personal commitment. With that, he put further thoughts out of his mind and enjoyed the ride along the river through the beautiful valley.

He stopped just before he left the south end of the valley at the cabin of Christopher Baker and his three wives, Sarah, Mary and Rebecca. Robert had had unusual feelings about Rebecca, the youngest of Christopher's wives, and when he saw her in the afternoon light these feelings were somewhere between total disbelief and utter enchantment and desire. Such feelings were totally foreign to him and he was not sure how to mask them from others.

This was exactly the reason he had moved out of the Baker household a few months earlier. When he was first sent to the St George area of the Mormon settlements over a year previously, he had been assigned residence at Christopher Baker's home. He had felt welcome and truly at home during this time. However, as these unusual feelings for Rebecca began to develop, his comfort level began to change, especially when Rebecca started casually meeting him at the stable on his returns from his daily tasks. At first, her attention to him went unnoticed by Christopher's two other wives, Sarah and Mary. But her leaving the cabin each afternoon, about the time Robert was to return, raised their suspicions of a developing relationship.

Mary had followed Rebecca out of the cabin late one afternoon and as she approached the stable, she observed Rebecca in the arms of Robert. Mary was a freethinking woman of the frontier and inwardly questioned the doctrine of the Church which permitted men multiple wives and women but one man. She understood Rebecca's attraction to Robert, as she herself had had similar but controlled feelings at various times in the past.

Mary debated at some length with herself how best to handle this attraction Rebecca now had for Robert. She realized it could lead to problems within the household and the Church itself, not to mention the damage it could do to Robert's sterling reputation. She decided she must speak to them both but wanted to select the proper timing for such a delicate conversation.

She selected the next time Christopher would be gone from the home site on a trip to town and when Robert would be returning. Two days later, she had her opportunity. Christopher had left for town shortly after lunch, announcing he would be returning after supper.

Mary made her move. She excused herself from Sarah and Rebecca and went to the stable a half hour or so before the general hour of Robert's return home, thus assuring herself she would already be there when he arrived. She positioned herself in one of the horse stalls hidden from the entrance to the stable itself and waited patiently.

She was not disappointed. Shortly, Rebecca arrived at the stable and struck an alluring pose in the entry. It was obvious to Mary that this pose had been practiced many times before. As Robert arrived, Mary held to her hidden position and watched with interest.

Mary felt her own heart skip again and again, as she observed the immediate welcoming deadlock of passion between the two of them. She watched as Robert's sultry gaze rested briefly of Rebecca's substantial breasts. For a brief moment, Mary fantasized herself there in Robert's arms, receiving the sensuous kisses he was now bestowing on Rebecca, but she conscientiously pushed these thoughts from her mind as she carefully choose the moment for her appearance.

Rebecca and Robert walked hand in hand toward the back of the stable and approached the stall hiding Mary. Mary intentionally stepped on a board at her feet, producing the sharp and brittle crack of weathered wood. With but a five second delay she backed out into their path. As she turned to gaze startlingly at them, Rebecca took a quick breath of astonishment. Even the air could not invade the silence. Robert's face tightened as the sobering reality of the situation and frightening possibilities flashed though his mind. The hot touch of the devil shot through Rebecca as she awaited even a whisper of emotion from Mary. They stood there, both gnawed with anxiety and sharing a terrible sense of humiliation.

Mary paused for a moment, as if hesitating about saying her thought. She shifted uneasily, then said, "It's just a good thing it was only I that saw all your carrying-ons and not Christopher." Then, noting their total embarrassment gave them a compassionate yet troubled look and waited for one of them to speak.

Looking at Rebecca, Robert admitted his seductive attraction to Rebecca was weak-willed and not at all proper for the real world of the Mormon Church. He would be leaving no later than week's end. His excuse, with Mary's blessing, would be that the restless man everyone knew him to be, was off to seek new horizons. They all sadly agreed that that solution seemed best and they all even further agreed to maintain a close, but careful future friendship with no mention ever, of the situation that had caused his departure from the Baker household.

So, as Robert now rode up after his visit with Brigham Young, his visit was appreciated and especially enjoyed by Christopher. Sarah, Mary and Rebecca were scurrying about the kitchen in preparation for dinner with their special guest.

Robert had an opportunity to discuss the strange reception he had experienced at the Brigham Young residence just a few hours earlier. As offering an explanation almost in the form of an apology, Christopher noted that an edict had been recently issued by the Elder's council that emigrants and non-Mormons in the area were not to receive further help or comfort as they passed through "Mormon country" on their way to California. In addition, any Mormon or his family aiding or providing food or comfort to these Gentiles would receive severe punishment by the Church. This meant a sure visit from the "Dantes".

Christopher went on to explain. Brigham Young had issued a recent ruling, involving all members of the church, to rededicate themselves to the principles and the work of the Church. A blood atonement edict had been issued. The letting of blood was now necessary to reach the life hereafter. Lack of cooperation or acceptance of these edicts would mean a visit from the "Dantes".

Robert had not previously heard the term "Dantes" and asked what and to whom it referred. Christopher explained, the "Dantes" were a secret enforcement group of men, most daring, adventurous, resolute, and hardened characters, generally selected by the Church's highest authority to carry out any vengeance they are assigned.

Whenever they are called upon by the heads of the Church to perpetrate some horrible act, they are encouraged and comforted by the leaders who tell them to go forward and obey the mandates they receive…. without inquiring whether their acts are right or wrong, and saying to them….. "The responsibility rests upon those who give those commands". Thus, the "Dantes" are like mere machines, which accept all commands in accordance with the will of God.

The "Dantes" recently had become more active in issuing punishment to non-conforming members of the Church and Gentiles who oppose the Church in any manner. A number of incidents had occurred recently throughout the territory.

One case involved an engineer named Custer who had signed a contract with Apostle Ezra Taft Benson to build a milldam on his property for $1,000. After the dam was finished, the debt remained unpaid, and the Mormon courts would not enforce the collection of the debt due the California emigrant. The engineer was loud and rash in pressing his claims and protesting his ill treatment.

Just before he was to leave for California, Mr. Custer was killed by the Indians, or the "Dantes". But it was well known that whoever did the deed were acting on the direction and wishes of the Church's Elders.....just as they had done in the Massacre of the Gunnison Survey party.

Another incident, of lesser extreme, was of Elder Whitlock, who lost his horses and cattle one night while making his way out of the territory. This incident implicated Apostle Ezra Taft Bensen, and more important, revealed that the Mormons already had adapted a general policy of blaming their misconduct, whenever possible, on the local Indians rather than on the "Dantes". Whitlock's loss had occurred one night while he camped near the Ezra Taft mill dam. All his cattle had been driven off in different directions during the night as a blind to prevent the discovery of the theft of his horses, making it appear as it the Indians had undertaken to steal his stock.

Robert's conversation with Christopher continued the next day, with additional news arriving by courier from Salt Lake City to the north. A number of political situations had occurred with the United States government that apparently had further caused Brigham Young to make some extreme speeches and suggestions, both as Governor of the Utah Territory and as President of the Church of Jesus Christ of Latter Day Saints. His threats and violent speeches spread quickly throughout the Mormon settlements and became common talk. Some of these speeches strongly suggested cutting off emigrants' heads or simply slitting their throats.

Christopher continued with what he had heard that very morning. He told of a trial held by the justice- of-the-peace in Harmony, the Mormon settlement just north. The trial was against a man who had otten into a fistfight with one of the

Elders. The justice said to the non Mormon, "If you ever lay hands on another Saint, I will have your head cut off before you leave this city. I thank God that the time is not far distant, and I shall rejoice when it comes that I shall have the authority to pass sentence of life and death upon the Gentiles, and I will have their heads snatched off like chickens in the barnyard."

Hearing this story, Robert grasp his neck gingerly as he recalled his actions with Rebecca just a few months previously.

It was obvious that the kind and gentle Mormons that Robert had first known in Hart's Bluff were changing and had decided not to provide any further aid and comfort to emigrants passing through or to the other Gentiles in the area.

The Church now referred to all non-Mormons as Gentiles. It also became painfully obvious that monies previously earned and still owed Robert for his services under the old contract, would not be paid.

He was more determined than ever to amplify and carry off his scam of accepting the Mormon teachings and further enhance his act that he was now a true Mormon. His life now definitely depended on it!!!!

Chapter 19

The Growing Urge to Escape....
Spring / Fall 1857

A rush of both anticipation and dread whirled inside Robert each time he devised a possible new or unique method of escape from this Church that had created hell on earth. His unmonitored and permitted medical trips to nearby settlements and to the Indian villages in the mountains presented him temporary freedom and his best opportunities.

Robert had a good sense for danger, and as he thought through his devised plans of escape, he was always on guard for holes in the plan; consequently, most of these plans were disposed of as just too risky or unworkable.

He was almost sure that his face at times betrayed a certain tension, the secret passion for escape, which he was attempting to hold rigidly under control. His mind was whirling with various thoughts, ideas and methods of escape. At night, he had difficulty sleeping, as thoughts raged through his brain on how to carry out his bold escape so he would not be stopped or even killed.

With a dazzling leap of logic, he concluded his best chances lay to the west rather than toward the east, since the east would be the escape route the Church would expect him to take.

He decided he would join the first caravan he could that was moving west through the territory. Selecting the right one would be risky in itself since most all were being watched carefully. However, he felt with his permitted travels he would be able to conjure up a believable story to aid his escape when he found the right one. He concluded a larger wagon trail would meet his criteria by offering a better opportunity to become "lost" in its numbers.

He continued his medical rounds to the Indian villages and Mormon settlements along the Spanish Trail leading from Salt Lake City to California. Each day he was prepared that this may be the day he discovered the correct caravan to join. He took with him his rifle, what little money he had been able to save, a picture of Elizabeth, his bed roll, his medical case, and little else so as not to raise any suspicion.

As he traveled into the mountains west of Cedar City, he encountered a small Pah-Vante tribe of Indians who he had previously met further north. He was always welcomed because of the "Good Medicine" he had performed on various members of the tribe.

Meeting with this small tribe again was of particular interest to Robert, primarily because of the chief's daughter, Running Deer, to whom Robert had taken a personal fancy. Running Deer had a fawn like beauty with the bloom of youth. Her hair was a plume of black gold falling to her waist. She was taller than most other Indian women, a vividly beautiful woman, whether Indian or white. Robert spent the better part of the day with the tribe, and as he departed for the Mormon settlement of Parowan that he now called "Home", he promised himself more frequent visits to see Running Deer.

He arrived just before sundown at his assigned residence at his old friend, Elder Black's home and while he wasn't at all pleased because what had happened between them on the trip to San Francisco, he had no choice in the matter. He felt he had been assigned to Elder Black's home so a closer eye could be kept on him.

Robert liked Brother Black's wife, Sadie, and enjoyed their three children, James, Martha and Larkin. The children made Robert's thoughts turn to his own family. Additionally, Robert had delivered James when he was born earlier than expected, on that Mormon wagon train to the "Promised Land" ten years previously.

Robert and James quickly developed a very strong bond over their mutual interest in medicine. Most evenings, the two would sit in front of the fireplace discussing various medical procedures. James's interest turned Robert's thoughts to himself at the same age and he was determined to do everything in his power to help kindle this interest in this young boy in hopes he would seek to follow it with a formal education.

This effort did not go unnoticed by Sadie, who showed her pleasure in Robert's actions with a frequent apple pie. Robert became endeared over the next few months to the Blacks who now saw him in a completely different light and truly liked what they saw. Eventually all barriers between Elder Black and Robert were forgotten and Elder Black actually became more human, Robert felt, than at anytime he had known him in the past.

With this increased trust, Robert had more freedom than previously, and was permitted to occasionally spend a night or two in outlaying settlements rather than having to return each evening. He welcomed this new freedom and was delighted that it had come as the result of his attitude change and that of becoming a "Mormon of convenience", just as he had planned.

Robert was now able to travel to the further settlements of Corn Creek, Fillmore and even as far as Buttermilk Fort, and into the mountains on either side of the Great Basin. He was able to spend more time in the various Indian villages and made frequent visits to Running Deer's village where he particularly enjoyed his welcome.

More numerous were the wagon trains that passed through the Mormon settlements as they traveled south along the Spanish Trail to seek their new fortunes in California territory. However, the settlements did not make the necessary passage through their territory easy for these Gentiles. The settlements all recalled the "Directives" that had come down from the Church's headquarters that help was not to be provided these "Non Believers", these "Gentiles" upon threat of personal harm to themselves. These directives spelled out details of considered support or help, which included selling any food provisions, livestock or gunpowder to them, and no trades of any kind were to be made.

This was a firm rule to be followed, in spite of the fact that the crops this spring had produced an abundant supply for the settlements.

Threats and violent speech against the emigrants were now common features of life in Salt Lake City according to reports received further south. Hearing such words and recognizing the threat of a visit from the "Dantes", all true members of the Church of Jesus Christ of Latter Day Saints would obey without question.

As one of the few doctors of medicine in the area, Robert did not take such threats to heart and remained true to the doctrine of medicine that he was to care for the sick wherever they were discovered. This brought him in contact with many of the trains passing through the area, and from each he learned more about their travels and experiences along the trail.

He learned that the Oregon Trail, east of Fort Bridger, was lined with wagons and that one would scarcely ever be out of sight of some wagon train. The destruction of property along the road was beyond description. Dust was very disagreeable but was nothing compared with the stench from dead animal carcasses, which lay along the trail and had died of fatigue and/or hunger.

Another observer noted that he had counted about a thousand wagons burned or discarded and about five hundred dead oxen. He thought the wagons had been burned to prevent them from being used by anyone else, yet had seen Mormon scavenger parties reaping a rich harvest. One party of emigrant Saints found over one hundred head of oxen wandering over the prairie, after checking ownership at Fort Bridger, added them to their teams.

The emigrant Saints also discovered that previous trains had buried valuable goods along the way, engraved with headboards on which was painted the name and age of the supposed deceased. Some such sites contained casks of brandy rather than bodies. This discovery encouraged them to dig and rummage even further. Some grave sites indeed contained just bodies and the Mormons gave resurrection to many in such a manner.

These stories further convinced Robert he must be extremely careful not to alter the rehearsed defense system he had devised as a "Mormon of convenience". His feelings toward the fanaticism of the Church were escalated into an immediate urgency to escape the Church's ever-increasing assault on human dignity, and their apparent disfigurement of most every facet of sane living.

Chapter 20

A Bolt to Freedom.......

Robert traveled the ten miles north from Corn Creek to the town of Fillmore. Fillmore had served briefly as the capital of the Utah territory and a red sandstone statehouse was the most notable feature of an otherwise barren town. A rather large wagon train arrived in Filmore that very day with a need for medical assistance. With hope in his heart, Robert rode the short distance to where the train was camped just outside of town. As he rode up, he was greeted warmly by most everyone he passed on the way to the wagon masters wagon. This seemed refreshing in itself after recent experiences.

When he asked one young boy where to find the wagon master, he was told to keep riding toward the center and look for a wagon with lots of children that would be the Fancher wagon. Robert found it with little problem. The Fancher family, consisting of the mother, father and eight children, was just settling down for their evening meal.

Robert introduced himself to Captain Alexander Fancher, a courtly southerner from Arkansas. His first impression of Captain Fancher was "Here is the human physical monument of a man with the awesome responsibility of Wagon Master but, also, that of father of eight children". Robert liked him immediately.

Robert was invited to partake of dinner with them and quickly accepted but mentioned he first wished to see the ill patient for whom he had been originally summoned.

As it happened, the young man was in a wagon nearby. He had been injured when he had been pulled from his horse and beaten by a gang of locals the previous day while riding through the town of Buttermilk Fort, just eight miles north. The young man had merely cast his eyes on a young Mormon girl of the settlement. While he had been badly beaten, all that was needed was a few of Doc Wood's surgical stitches since nothing was broken and a few days rest would be all that was required.

The boy's injuries, and how they had happened, became the subject of discussion as Robert sat down to the late dinner Captain Fancher's wife, Eliza, had saved for him.

It was of no surprise that the train had had no success in replenishing their supplies since leaving Fort Bridger, and additionally, that they had been falsely accused of poisoning a water hole as they passed through Pleasant Grove, about 40 miles north. Captain Fancher blamed that false accusation for their not being able to purchase the supplies they badly needed.

Robert assured him that that was only one of the problems and related some of the other reasons the members of the Church were not sympathetic, even hostile, to the needs of the "Gentiles" passing through their territory. As the evening wore on, Robert had the opportunity to tell his full story and noted he had virtually become an unwilling prisoner of the area with but one desire, to escape.

As Robert arose in the camp the next morning, a group of men and women were gathered at one of the nearby wagons having a discussion with a man Robert had seen before in his travels. As Robert approached the group, the man he recognized approached Robert with his hand outstretched and a smile on his face. He introduced himself as Robert Aden and explained they had met when Dr. Wood was involved in the Avian Cholera outbreak years before. Aden further explained that he had joined the wagon train, just outside Salt Lake City when he heard they were in need of extra hands to manage their large herd of horses they were moving to California. It had not been the money offered that enticed him to join the wagon train, but rather the opportunity to leave this "never, never land of make believe".

Robert recognized that he and Aden were kindred spirits of sorts, and like a lightning bolt, Robert's mind was made up. This was the wagon train he had been seeking to make his own escape.

That evening he was welcomed into the group at a special central gathering, with fiddling, dancing and something reminiscent of Tarantula juice. As Robert drifted off to sleep that night, his last thoughts were that these people were more human, more natural, more like he was. He truly relished the feeling of contentment brought on by his decision to join up with them.

In the next few days before leaving Fillmore, Robert became acquainted with many more of the people on the train. When he learned, there were two families with the last name Wood, he went immediately to seek them out.

He found them with little difficulty. Solomon Wood was 38 years old, about the same age as Robert. He and his wife Martha had two boys, James, 18 and John, 11. Solomon's brother, William, was in the next wagon with his wife, Melinda. They had three boys, Thomas, 10, Sylvester, 9 and James Irvine, 8.

Surprisingly, after comparing ancestry, they determined they were indeed related: cousins who had never corresponded or even knew of each other's existence. Their fathers were brothers, both born in England, who had come to Philadelphia together when both were in their teens. Robert's father had married and moved to New York while their father had elected to seek his fortune in the rich farmlands further inland and to the south.

Doc Wood was quickly accepted and Robert learned many things about the various people on the train and of its final destination.

He learned this train, undoubtedly, was the richest and best equipped train that ever crossed the Rocky Mountains. They were going to settle in California, in a location that had already been selected and claimed by Captain Baker, or known fondly as "Uncle Jack". "Uncle Jack" had made at least two previous trips into this area on his way to California and was now returning with his wife and seven children.

Robert's first opportunity to show his usefulness to his newly adopted friends and his new found relatives came as the train approached the community of Corn Creek. The Corn Creek settlement was an Indian farm, one of several throughout the area, under the supervision of the United States government appointed Indian agent, Garland Hurt. He was one of the few who still remained in the territory. While Agent Hurt, whom Robert knew well, was not present, it made little difference. Robert knew many of the Indians themselves, as well as their leaders. With Robert's help, the wagon train was successful in obtaining thirty bushels of corn, all that the Indians had to spare.

Robert proved his usefulness again as the train passed through Parowan. Sadie, Brother Black's wife, was an independent thinking woman and was kindhearted and different than most of the other Mormon wives. Even so, Robert approached her with some trepidation to ask her to sell some eggs and some flour to the hungry emigrants. She did so, even at the risk of physical punishment and the possible raft of the heavens that may be bestowed upon her by her husband, an Elder of the Church, should he find out.

She told Robert she would keep secret the fact that he was with the wagon train. She knew that it would not be at all acceptable to her husband because of his pledge to carefully watch Robert's activities and also because of his "standing" in the Church and the duty she knew he felt.

Chapter 21

Gathering Clouds...

The wagon train moved slowly through the stunted grass and scrub brush that ended only where trees of the far distance mountains reached down to greet the prairie. Mile after mile only a slight undulation here and there broke the monotony of the landscape as they passed through the Great Basin.

The evenings began to grow cooler and the evening fires comforting. As the men sat around the flickering fire, many stories were exchanged both by the emigrants themselves and by those who had joined the wagon caravan since it had entered Mormon country. The stories that were related explained much to Robert, and Robert's stories, and those of others, much to the emigrant's understanding of what they had been facing from the Mormon communities since leaving Fort Bridger.

Robert Aden, who had joined the train as it passed through Salt Lake City, had the more interesting and frightening stories. He told of the new growing strength of the Mormon Church and how they had outgrown their discretion and took to murdering emigrants who did not belong to their denomination, and robbing trains and killing people passing through their area.

Robert recalled on one occasion while he was living with a Mormon family, that a horse with a bloody saddle was brought into the corral, the blood washed off and the horse added to the Mormon's herd. At the time, Robert thought that it had been the blood on one of the Gentiles, but had said nothing that would jeopardize getting a bullet or otherwise have threatened his pretentious life as the pretend Mormon he had become.

Other tales were related that explained the secret of polygamy by the Mormons: one man, ten wives each having three to five children. In twenty years, the Mormons would be strong enough to protect themselves from the gentiles, the intrusion into the Church's affairs by the United States government, and their appointment of non-Mormons to various offices within the territory, who the Mormons considered just damn rascals,

Long into the evening, the discussions continued as small bits of recent news were shared. One such news item was that Brigham Young was considering creating martial law to counteract the actions of the U.S. government, which wished to send troops to aid and protect the caravans passing through the Mormon territory. Another bit of news told of the incredible aspects of the "Reformation Proclamation" that had been imposed by Prophet Young. That proclamation noted that the atonement for sin could only be accomplished by the sinner's throat being cut or otherwise being forced to give up their lives as a consequence of their sin.

It was truly viewed as an act of loving kindness to shed the sinner's blood in order to save his soul from eternal damnation. Further, that this was a form of ritual murder the Church implicitly endorsed, as had also been endorsed by Christ himself in the Gospels.

On and on the stories were told….. Of the 2,500 soldiers who were now on their way from the East and the 500 mobocrats from California. The mobocrats were a group of volunteers who had suffered indignities and starvation at the hands of the Mormons as they had previously passed through Mormon territory.

These soldiers and mobocrats were to bring Mormons back under the control of the U.S. government. No longer would the Mormons be able to print their own money, have plural marriages or dictatorial powers over the citizens of the area, nor charge fees to wagon trains passing through.

The story told by Richard Aden was the most unsettling to the group gathered around the fire that night. He told them he had learned that the Church had determined that the "Fancher Wagon Train" had the very rifle that had killed Joseph Smith back in Missouri years before, and that some of the men involved with the killing were, indeed, also with the train.

This further explained much of the antagonized and highhanded treatment they had received upon entering the Mormon territory. However, the stories were completely untrue, just as the story was untrue that they had poisoned a watering hole during one of their stops just outside Salt Lake City. The Fancher party had held their peace each time new accusations had been hurled their way.

Clouds that formed in the night sky grew more ominous and the darkness seemed to deepen to total black as the fire died and each individual returned to their specific wagon, with their own deep thoughts, for a restless attempt at a night's sleep.

Chapter 22

A Time to Rest and Rejuvenate........

Late Summer 1857

The next morning it was difficult for Captain Fancher to get the train up and moving. The size alone made the job difficult, but the fact that they were all weary, dirty, and hungry made the job even more difficult.

It was a one hundred fifty-person train: sixty men, forty women, fifty children, six hundred to nine hundred finest cows, oxen enough to haul forty to sixty heavy wagons, twenty to thirty thoroughbred horses, plus a sizable herd of regular horses.

This was perhaps the wealthiest train to have passed through Mormon Country, especially considering the valuable furniture items and considerable sums of ready cash in silver and bills that had been, carefully hidden throughout the wagons. Captain Fancher figured the train's total value between $75,000 and $100,000. His brother, who had been this way before, put the value at twice that..... Even more upon reaching their destination in California.

When Captain Fancher announced that this would be the last day of travel before a welcome rest, there was instant excitement and joy throughout the wagon train. They had had enough of the Mormons' Great Basin that they had been traveling through for days upon days, and of the Mormons that lived there.

At the rim of the Great Basin, just a day's travel ahead, there lay a narrow strip of open, well- watered grassland known as Mountain Meadows.   It was the ideal location to rest themselves, their horses, and cattle before setting out on the arduous trek across the dry desert to southern California.

Little did the Fancher train know that the Mormon Church leaders were also considering this remote site, far removed from prying eyes of strangers, for some of their own religious consecration.

On Friday, the fourth of September, an hour or so before sunset, they entered the narrow five mile long valley and passed by Elder Jacob Hamblin's ranch house and his nearby spring . Doc Wood knew this area well, having been through there a number of times. The wagon train descended a short distance along the opposite slope from the cabin and made camp for the night before it grew completely dark.

The next morning was a leisurely one but by midday they moved two or three miles further south, finally halting at a spot thirty or forty yards to the north of a second and larger spring which was in a shallow depression six feet below the valley floor.

Within a short time, a more permanent camp was made. The livestock were turned out to graze on the fall meadow grass. Water was carried to the campsite and as dusk set in, the travelers were in preparation of a frugal, but welcome dinner.

That Saturday night, they gathered around the campfires feeling relieved at finally being beyond the power of the strange, frenzied people that they had encountered along the trail since Fort Bridger.

Robert had assumed relief of many of the weary men on sentry duty. Additionally, he continued the handling of various medical problems and other necessary duties as the train moved into the Mountain Meadows area. He too needed this few days rest before starting the arduous journey through the desert to California. Robert felt relieved as well, having apparently made his escape from Mormon captivity.

The plan for the group was to stay a week, permitting their animals to graze and restore their strength. This would then permit a speedier trip across the desert where the watering holes were fifty or more miles apart. Even though their rations were already low, they felt the speedier desert crossing would make up for the extra supplies they would consume with their delay.

They were somewhat worried about the Indians of the desert, which they had heard were friendlier to the Mormons than to the Gentiles passing through. Captain Fancher alleviated these concerns, somewhat, by pointing out that they had forty or fifty sharpshooters in their ranks and the Pah-Ute Indian braves of southern Utah were known to have few if any firearms, and to be one of the least aggressive and warlike tribes in the entire territory. Robert confirmed these facts from his own personal knowledge.

In spite of the fact, the entire wagon train was feeling a great deal safer than they had in any of the pervious weeks, they followed the established rule throughout the trip, sentries were posted around the outer perimeter of the camp and the train settled down for a peaceful night's sleep.

Early daybreak Sunday morning, Robert and a new acquaintance, who also was about to finish his sentry duty for the night, were exchanging greetings and short stories. Robert's laughter stopped as though a valve in his chest had closed. He sat back with a look of total surprise as blood suddenly arose like a jet from his new acquaintances head in response to a distant rifle shot that also destroyed the tranquility of the ever-brightening morning.

Robert instinctively followed the sound of the shot with his eyes, just in time to catch the sight of a small group of Indians on the top of a low hill to the west.

Before he was able to sound a further alarm, six more shots rang out, two of which hit other early risers this fateful morning. Shouting quickly erupted throughout the camp, alerting everyone to impending danger. Out of the wagons, crept men with their rifles in their hands, still dressed in their nightshirts. Women and children could be seen peering out from under the covers of the wagons.

The attack was so sudden that all the sharp shooters of the wagon train could do was watch as whooping savages tumbled down the slope and ran off the livestock that had been leisurely grazing in the fields some distance from the train itself. A state of confusion held the wagon train's occupants motionless for a matter of minutes before Captain Fancher shouted orders that were quickly relayed throughout the train to assure the safety of those just awakening.

The men worked frantically, shoving the heavy schooners and carriages to form a huge corral. The sharp shooters, with their long rifles, stood facing the direction of the initial assault while searching the low hills for any movement.

As the last wagon was moved into place to complete the closure of the corral, the main band of savages charged down the mountainside yelling and shooting. Rifles barked back from the train. The attackers hesitated before this vicious response and fell back. The wagon train used the next period of time to further dig in and to chain the wheels of the wagons together. Others feverishly dug with picks and shovels to throw up a breastwork defense.

Soon, a coffee aroma permeated the wagons and an uneasy calm settled over the area, as both the attacks and the gunshots ceased.

The morning sun rose in the sky and with it, brought intense heat. When it reached midday, it became almost unbearable and the train was running out of water.

Robert was busy treating the wounded. Six or seven men had been killed outright, and ten or so had been wounded. He discovered his new acquaintance had been shot through the right eye and that the bullet had torn off the backside of his head upon its exit. His new friend had died instantly. Robert could not help but feel that, as easily as not, this victim could have been him. With the increased heat of the midday and the lack of water, his wounded patients' temperatures were becoming dangerously high.

Without water, the emigrants of the train could not hold out. Water was but a short three hundred to four hundred feet beyond the wagon corral. Captain Fancher called for volunteers to access the water and bring a bucket or two back to the enclosure. Three men stepped forward without hesitation. With buckets in hand, they were to slither, one at a time, to the well and return with as much water as possible.

When the first to leave seeking water was shot fifteen feet outside the corral and the second but five feet outside the corral, a different plan would have to be adopted.

After considerable thought, and as the desperate need for water grew, it was decided they would send two children to the well. They reasoned that the savages would not shoot the children, especially if they were girls. However, the idea of sending two girls to the well did not set well with the group. It was then that two eight or ten year old boys volunteered to dress in girls white garments and dance hand in hand to the well for water. As they left the compound, the air was totally still as everyone held their breath. It worked! The boys made two trips each with two buckets during the next few hours. As they prepared for their third trip to the well, their mothers had some ominous feelings that they would be pushing their luck and held tightly to their boys, but soon relented. The boys were but twenty feet outside the safety of the corral when they were both shot dead. Tighter water rationing would have to be continued until a better solution could be reached.

Some of the men took up their shovels and picks and began to dig a well within the compound itself. After digging for three or four hours, the task was given up as a failure.

Surely, since they were on one of the main trails to California, their plight would soon be recognized and help would arrive, if it were not already on its way!

On the evening of the third day, the Indians made their most determined attack. Sneaking down through the gullies, they circled the train, shooting with intensively until dusk. The tall grass provided the attackers some protection from the return fire of the sharp shooters with their long rifles. Nonetheless, the Indians felt the full accuracy of the sharp shooters and fell back into the hillsides, carrying their wounded with them.

It was now obvious that their plight had not been reported and that no help was coming. At their council meeting late that afternoon, it was decided they no longer could remain in their defensive position and that they must now send someone for help to the nearest settlement if they expected to survive.

William Aden fearlessly volunteered to make his way north to seek the assistance from another emigrant train that had been following them a few days behind, or to go all the way to Cedar City, if necessary, for help. Robert quickly became the second volunteer. He argued that he knew the area well and also had many friends in Cedar City to whom he could appeal.

Chapter 23

The Dastardly Deed…..

The two stole off into the dark night, leading their horses several miles until they could safely mount them. Galloping toward Cedar City, it was not long before they saw a campfire that they surmised was the wagon train they were seeking.

Robert hung back as William Aden cautiously approached the campfire. Aden dismounted to greet the three men who rose to greet him. One, a Mormon Elder named Stewart, asked Aden what he wanted. The other two Mormons, Benjamin Arthur and Joel White, listened as Aden related the attack in the meadow.

Robert, watching from a distance, observed that just as Aden finished his story, Stewart drew his pistol, put it to Aden's breast, and killed him on the spot.

Robert quickly turned his horse to flee and, in doing so, became noticed for the first time. He galloped his horse toward the safety of the nearest ravine. He was almost there when he felt a shot enter his back.

The shot almost knocked him from his horse, but he clung to the saddle horn and quickly escaped into the dark.

He contemplated his next move. Should he attempt to continue toward Cedar City or turn back, the shorter distance, to the Fancher wagon train?

To ride toward Cedar City would take him across open prairie in daylight, where he could be spotted by those intent on stopping him. In his quickly weakening condition, he also felt that he may not make the longer trip and would leave the emigrants of the train hoping they had gotten through and relief would be coming. Therefore, the return to the wagon train, to provide a warning of pending disaster, seemed the better solution.

A few hours before dawn, after slowly picking his way through the ravines and tree-covered mountains to avoid any further encounters with either Mormons or Indians, he arrived back to the corral exhausted and almost falling from his mount. His whole right side was now caked with dried blood, and fresh blood was still erupting from his wound. A couple of the sentries quickly helped him from his horse and laid him on the ground.

He, weakly and with broken voice, relayed his story and the incident surrounding the death of Aden at the campsite of Mormons. Most who gathered around Robert discounted his encounter as a figment of his feverish imagination due to his wounds. Robert had no remaining strength to further convince them and shortly fell unconscious.

When he awoke hours later, he was in the wagon, a patient himself. In spite of his wounds, he knew he was in better condition than most of the other wounded. He had found water during his dangerous trip outside the compound. Some of the women who had previously worked with him dressed his wound as best they could and further provided him comfort.

This day was to be the worst of all. Many of the wounded of the wagon train were actually dying of thirst and there was nothing that could be done to alleviate the situation. The entire caravan was weak from lack of water. By midday, the stink of the newly dead and those who had died in the preceding day's attacks and remained unburied, began to permeate the compound.

Again, an effort was made to obtain water from the outside well, but only one trip by a younger man who ran zig zaggedy, both to and from the well, proved a success. He arrived back inside the compound with only half-full buckets, since much of the water had splashed out during his run. It was decided to wait until dark and try again. However, the savages were waiting at the well site, having themselves arrived just after dark, and the young runner's screams could be heard throughout the valley as the savages took their revenge.

The morning of the fifth day dawned on the weary compound. Their energy to resist was crumbling rapidly as were their numbers themselves. Their ammunition was nearly gone and so was their food. The stench of their unburied remained in their nostrils, and all were experiencing the agony of thirst. Their further ability to withstand attacks was no longer a question to be answered. It had now become just a matter of time before the end.

Chapter 24

A Twinkling of Hope......

They prayed for relief from this torment, while at the same time, praying for the strength to continue their resistance. This was merely wishful thinking, since no relief was on the way and all their resistance was crumbling rapidly.

Suddenly, a cry of a sentry shook them from their stupor. Two men, mounted on horses and bearing a white flag, were advancing toward the compound. In a twinkling, utter despair turned to weak cheering for what appeared to be the answer to their most reverent prayers.

The horsemen came on at a slow walk, taking seemingly forever to reach the compound. Finally, a square-shaped man, with an air of authority dismounted and smiled at the group greeting him, as it crowded toward him. His companion, William Bateman by name, remained on his horse, holding the white flag. As Captain Fancher stepped forward, the stranger took his hand and introduced himself as John D. Lee, Indian Commissioner for the district.

The group pressed closer to him to hear what he had to say. He told Captain Fancher, with a slow grave voice, that the Paiute Indians were rebellious and had become difficult to handle, but declared he felt sure he could persuade them to parley. As the discussion continued between the men of the wagon train and John Lee, he gained the group's complete confidence.

While Robert could not see all that was going on from the wagon of the sick and wounded, he could hear the louder discussions amongst the men of the wagon train, and became bewildered by this turn of events.

After much more discussion, the Indian Commissioner and the white flag holder rode back the way they had come, but with the entire compounds hopes and prayers for his successful parley with the menacing Indians.

He was gone two hours. He came back with a wagon following in his dust. Again, a group circled him for the results of his parley. He told them that the Indians had agreed to let them go, if they would but surrender their arms.

Upon hearing this, it caused a major stir amongst the men of the compound. Most objected and exclaimed they would need them for their protection further on the trail. John Lee stood firm and explained calmly and carefully, that this was the only way that further attacks could cease.

Groups of men discussed the ramifications of this proposal, and finally recognizing that they had little choice since, they were practically out of ammunition, their food and water gone, and there was no hope of surviving another day of attacks. As some looked at their wives and children some distance away, and seeing their despair and suffering, they came to the full realization that there could be no other answer but to comply with the Indians' terms.

It took almost a half an hour to unchain the wagons from each other, remove the other barriers, and move one wagon out of the way in order to permit the wagon that had followed in Lee's dust to be brought into the compound. Slowly the wagon train's rifles were placed on the bed of the wagon. As the last of the rifles clattered to the bed of the wagon, John D. Lee smiled grimly and nodded to the driver. The wagon rumbled off over the low rise to the west. Back came a group of white men on horses to protect the wagon train from further attacks, just as had been promised by Lee.

These men were greeted with cheering. While some members of the wagon train appeared deeply distressed, and others were in tears, all felt their happy deliverance had come. Robert, in his weakened condition, was not so sure.

One wagon was loaded with all the youngest children. The wagon with all the sick and wounded was to follow. Off the group went, under the protection of the newly arrived "protectors".

Robert had positioned himself so he could view the activity from the back of the wagon in which he was riding. The two wagons led off to the north end of the valley, the women followed, walking behind the second wagon. Some distance behind the women, the men walked in a single line between a spacing of the protecting troopers on either side, and moved more slowly.

The distance between the faster walking women and the men grew greater. Momentarily, the men were lost from Robert's sight, over a rise in the floor of the mountain meadow below. His rather half consciousness was awakened to full alertness at the sound of rifle fire coming from the direction of the men out of sight.

Shortly, he could see the men below. They were being attacked by the troops that had been trusted to protect them, and now they were totally defenseless. Almost immediately upon this revelation, the full effect of exactly what was going on, hit Robert with a dark premonition of things to come and held him still, but alert.

Chapter 25

"War Paint" and White Skins......

A woman's scream chilled him to the marrow. The scream was followed by Indians shrieking, shooting, and yelling as they leaped down the nearby slopes on both sides of the column of the walking women, the wagon containing the children, and the wagon transporting Robert and the other wounded. For a moment Robert froze, with an open mouth and wide open eyes, as he saw the slaying of one of the women. This initial shock was short lived as painted Indian warriors began to enter the front of the wagon of the defenseless sick and wounded.

The throat of the first woman at the front of the wagon was slit and a gurgling scream clawed its way out of her throat. The wounded man beside her was hit with a tomahawk squarely on the top of his head, splitting it side to side. Robert's one fleeting strange thought was, "No scalp trophy left for this warrior".

This brought Robert back to life from the developing nightmare, and in spite of his wounds, moved him to action.

With his adrenaline level rising, he turned to the young pregnant woman beside him in the wagon who appeared to be starting into labor. He almost tossed her out of the back of the wagon and immediately followed her. He shouted over the din of the ongoing action and screamed, "Follow me and run".

Robert had observed a small outcrop of willow bushes on a small rise about thirty feet to the west of the wagon, and they headed in that direction. Almost there, Robert looked back toward the wagon containing the children, and with a quick glance at the women that had been walking behind the wagons observed that blood lusting was at a fever pitch in both places.

As they reached the willow brushes, both Robert and the young woman fell exhausted into the middle of the outcropping, somewhat hiding them from the action around them. Robert's wounds had been reopened with his exertion and he was bleeding profusely. The young pregnant woman was having difficultly breathing and was holding tightly to her stomach as if to squeeze out the pain that she was feeling. Robert knew the extra excitement and exertion had brought on her labor and that she was just minutes short of giving birth.

Robert knew she would have to remain very quiet so not to be discovered by the Indians nearby, but he recognized it as a most difficult task for a woman in the labor of childbirth. With the rapid loss of blood he was now experiencing, he also wondered how he could provide his services to her as a physician.

As they lay there in the brush, Robert's mind was taken off his current predicament as he watched through the willows the slaughter that was going on by the Indians of the women of the wagon train and of the older children in the lead wagon. It became immediately apparent that all the women were to be killed. In closer observance, he noted that the Indians were selecting only the older children for their dastardly deed.

From over the low rise of the meadows' floor, he could see the ongoing slaughter of the men with whom he had become acquainted such a short time before. No mercy was being spared by this vicious attack. The screams of the Indians and of the victims sent chills up and down his spine. One fleeting thought was that these screams might mask any that would come from the pregnant woman laying there in the brush alongside him. Thankfully, she was now unconscious and had not observed the same evil to which he had been privy.

It was then that a small group of painted Indians passed directly in front of their hiding place. Robert crunched even lower to hide himself amongst the thick willow outgrowth while still attempting to keep his eyes on the action passing before him. His eyes opened wide with astonishment as he recognized two of the painted Indians passing in front of him. He knew them not as Indians, but as Mormons of the Church of Jesus Christ of Latter Day Saints. He had been to their homes and treated their families on various occasions over the past few years. At first sighting, Robert was not sure it truly was them because of the "war paint" they had on their faces and bodies. However, their white skin and blond hair gave them away.

His mind flashed back to his encounter a few nights before at the camp when Aden and he had found Elder Stewart, Benjamin Arthur and Joel White. Where Steward had drawn his pistol, put it to Aden's breast, and killed him on the spot and he, himself, had barely escaped with but a shot in the back. It was true, the Mormons, along with a hostile, renegade Paiute group of Pah-Vante Indians, were the culprits in this dastardly deed that was being spread out before his eyes.

No sooner than he had this realization, the pregnant woman awoke and gave a loud, guttural moan. This stopped the passing group of Mormons and Paiute Indians in their tracks.

One Paiute peered into the willow thicket, and with his war spear, moved some of the heavy branches apart. He immediately observed the woman in her dirt clad white dress, and thrust his spear forward into her midsection. The Indian then followed his spear into the thicket, raising his tomahawk to finish the job.

As the tomahawk was being wielded toward the woman's head, with his last waning strength Robert grasped the hand of the Indian to stop the blow, but to no avail. The blow struck home and ended both the life of the woman and her unborn baby that Robert had hoped to save. With an almost involuntary springing backhand, the Paiute Indian pushed the tomahawk toward Robert. It caught Robert in the left temple and sent him reeling onto his back.

The last thing Robert was to recall, before he passed out, was the painted Indian bending over him with knife in hand, and feeling his scalp being cut and pulled from his head, along with a loud shrill Indian victory war cry.

Chapter 26

The Scavengers Cometh….

Maybe it was the next day, possibly even two or three days later, when Robert was to regain even the slightest consciousness.

He felt himself being dragged feet first out of the thicket. By whom, he did not know, but regardless, he could offer no resistance. In his semi consciousness, he felt the warmth of the sunshine on his upturned face. While his mind was far from alert, he did recognize voices around him. Something about his boots, which he felt being removed. Shortly thereafter, he felt himself being lifted onto the hard bottom of a wagon and covered completely with various items of clothing which blotted out the rays of the warm sun.

Robert's next memory was of lying on a straw bed, apparently in a barn. He was to learn later that Jacob Hamblin had found him lying outside the willow outcropping, and that he was hardly recognizable with blood-socked shirt and blood caked face and head. Truly, Robert's fine boots made the difference in where he could have been and where he ended up.

When Jacob saw the boots, he knew instantly they belonged to Doc Wood, and that must be the good Doc under that heavy matting of blood and dirt. It was Jacob who had placed Robert in the wagon and covered him with blankets and other articles of clothing that was being salvaged from the "battle field". Jacob realized that if others knew Robert had been with the train at the time of the attack, he would surely also be killed to leave no tell tale evidence behind to identify the deed that had been done.

No one knew of Robert's survival except Jacob, himself, and his wife. She was a simple-minded person of about forty-five and looked with the eyes of her husband at everything. Both knew they were wrong in the eyes of the Church and other friends by caring for Robert in his time of need, but the recent circumstances and actions of the Church had softened their convictions.

Jacob Hamblin's home was at the north end of Mountain Meadows, and Robert had been called there a number of times due to various accidents and sicknesses that had occurred in the past few years. Jacob had developed a fondness for Robert because of this service. He felt sure there must be a very good reason Robert was with the wagon train at the time of the onslaught. They also knew that their own lives would be in jeopardy should others of the Mormon community discover they were harboring a survivor of the recent action.

During the next few days, Robert had the faint recollection of overhearing voices saying that all the dead bodies of the emigrants had been stripped naked and the clothing, along with the wagons had been taken to Cedar City where they were auctioned off. All profits went into the till of the Church... and the gold, found hidden in the fake flooring of various wagons, went directly into the Church treasury. The supporting Indians mostly took the cattle, horses, rifles and food items from the emigrants' wagons. The seventeen surviving children under the age of seven where adopted by various Mormon families, to be raised as their own. Robert had difficultly comprehending all this chatter.

The Hamblins recognized that they must do something to better hide Robert from possible discovery. It was then they confided in a Snake Indian boy of about seventeen, called

Albert Hamblin, whom they had been raising as their own son for about ten years. From past visits by Robert to the ranch, Jacob had learned that Robert was well acquainted with the boy's tribe.

They decided that Albert would take Robert by Indian travois, into the mountains to the west and on further north to the tribe of his ancestors who, they felt, would welcome the opportunity to care for Robert until he, hopefully, returned to full health. They truly questioned if Robert's recovery was at all possible because of the serious condition in which they knew him to be.

In the back of their minds, they wondered if Robert would even survive the trip into the mountains with Albert. However, it was the best they could do for Robert under the present circumstances, and he would go with their blessings.

Chapter 27

It must be Heaven....

The next morning, at first light, Robert was placed on the travois that had been provided by Arthur, the Pah-Vante Indian boy. Robert was covered with various blankets and clothing items, to conceal him from possible discovery, until their final destination was reached. Jacob Hamblin told Arthur to keep Robert fully covered, and if stopped by anyone and asked what and where he was going, to reply that he was merely taking some of the recently acquired booty to share with one of the friendly Indian tribes.

The travois bounced along over raised rocks and mounds of earth, making the journey very painful for Robert. He would fall in and out of consciousness numerous times during this difficult journey. Occasionally, he would feel Arthur's presence and hear his voice anxiously trying to assure that he was still alive and to give him some refreshing water. Robert lost all sense of time.

He awoke after an unknown period of time, with the soft voice attempting to speak to him. Slowly, hesitantly, he partially opened his eyes, and observed a strong light and something hovering over him, gently speaking words he could not comprehend. In his sickly and weakened humor, he thought this must be Heaven, and that this was an angel sent to comfort and care for him. He was to learn, a number of weeks later that his first thoughts were not too far from the truth.

When Robert finally awoke, he found he was in doeskin clothing on a bed of pine bowers on the left side of a teepee. In the middle of the teepee was a small fire. Robert watched with fascination as the smoke from the fire wound its way through the open flap at the top of the teepee into the cooler night air. Across the teepee on the other side of the fire, was another bed similar to the one he was now laying on. Where was he??? He could remember very little of what had happened to him.

Shortly, the front flap of the teepee opened and he saw, first a hand, and then a dark-skinned body coming through the opening. He had regained enough of his faculties to realize it was his favorite Indian squaw, Running Deer.

Running Deer had taken him into her teepee and was providing the care that only an Indian woman could. She had learned well from her ancestors, who had long been the medicine men of the tribe of which she was now an integral part.

Arthur came in the next morning before he left to return home. Running Deer and Arthur conversed at considerable length as he related to her what had happened to the wagon train in the valley and what he knew of Robert's plight and of his condition. While Robert could understand a portion of their discussion, his mind was not alert enough to understand all that had been said in the Pah-Vante language. Nevertheless, he understood clearly, as Running Deer gazed across the fire at him that she considered this broken shell of a man "her returning warrior". He, then and there, willingly accepted his fate and whatever challenges were to come, knowing his struggling spirit and weakened body could resist no more.

The winter months were but a confused memory to Robert. By spring of the New Year, he began to regain some of his faculties and set foot outside the teepee for the first time since his arrival in the Indian village. Running Deer and the rest of the small tribe had cared for him as one of their own during the harsh winter months.

In his halted discussions with Running Deer, he learned a great deal about his condition. He slowly began to recall the initial shooting and many other incidences leading up to his present condition. Running Deer related other details to him about how he had gotten to the village, and just how ill he had been all winter.

From what he learned, he concluded that he must have received a severe concussion during the attack. He put his hands up to feel his head. The curvature of the cranium was abnormal, with ridges where bone mass had been misaligned and had now somewhat healed into a notable deformity.

While feeling his head, he missed the feel of his once curly hair on the top of his head. This had been replaced with scar tissue. With his first experience at regaining his humor, he thought to himself, "At least I have retained some of my original waves, even though in place of my hair, it is now the new wavy scar tissue from the effects of my cracked cranium". Giving a slight chuckle, he was thankful for Running Deer and was just happy he was still alive.

He learned that the Indian treatment for his condition, though primitive to him, was every bit as successful as would his professional treatment have been, had he been able to treat himself. His gunshot wounds had been stuffed with various herbs that the Indian squaws had gathered from the surrounding area, at Running Deer's direction, just before the first snow had come last fall.

His scalp had been treated with heavy applications of buffalo grease, and rest and quiet had been used for his concussion.

Running Deer told him that other herbs were placed in broth that she had given him many times each day, until such time as he began to eat on his own. Robert surmised these herbs were something that helped thin his blood to keep it from clotting. She told him, also, that she had to have some of the tribe's squaws and braves take turns holding him down at various times, since he was hostile and would not stay calm and quiet as she wanted him to do.

Robert was totally humbled by such devotion and attention provided during his recovery to this point. He realized he had a long way to go to regain his strength and previous weight. He was determined to repay his care in any manner he possibly could. However, thoughts of just how this could be accomplished were driven from his head by exhaustion and fatigue. He would have to think about it another day.

Chapter 28

Robert...The Mountain Man 1858

As early spring waned into early summer, Robert's strength began returning slowly. He found he could make short hunting trips with some of the Indian braves. He learned a great deal from them and quickly discovered how he could begin to repay for his care. He could help provide food and other necessities for the tribe.

He learned to use a bow and arrow. With lots of practice, he learned to shoot almost as well as the braves themselves. He was determined to obtain a rifle or two for his tribe, since they now had none, and a rifle would definitely make their job of hunting much easier.

As Robert's strength permitted, he began exploring the surrounding mountains and valleys by himself, and in a surprising way, found the singular experience a welcome change. During the early summer months, he became proficient at trapping beaver and killing deer, elk and other small animals that lived in the area. Catching a rattlesnake by its tail became almost a ritual and a right of passage into the tribe. Many times, he would quickly skin the rattler and eat it raw, just as the Indians had been doing for centuries.

With patience, and by working beside the squaws of the village, he learned to skin all kinds of animals and to tan and soften the hides. He became more fluent with the language of this particular tribe and that of two or three other tribes of the area.

On one singular hunting trip in July, Robert discovered a small spring where the water entering the small pool would create small bubbles. It was the bubbles that first attracted him to the spring. The water was crystal clear and had an unusual taste of purity. Robert knew from his previous knowledge that such waters also contained a number of healthful minerals. The spring was but a short distance from the tribe's current location and after marking the site well, he returned to the village to report his discovery to the tribe's chief.

A small group consisting of the chief, the chief's son, Flying Eagle, Robert, himself, and his squaw, Running Deer, set off the next morning to further investigate the mystical waters. As they approached the area of the springs, they were stopped by an instinctive, yet uneasy, awareness of impending danger.

They exchanged glances as they heard the ferocious growl of a nearby bear. Almost immediately, the bear attacked Flying Eagle, who was the closest to the brush from which the bear had emerged. With one swipe of his claws, the bear flung Flying Eagle into the air as if he were a toy. Flying Eagle landed on the ground, a few steps in front of the group.

The bear, ignoring the others standing motionless, moved forward and began to claw ferociously at Flying Eagle's head. Robert, as if awakening from a trance, jumped forward and onto the back of the bear, just as the bear's jaws were opening to finish the job it had started.

Robert began riding the bear, as one would ride a wild horse. With one hand, he hung on to the long hairs on the back of the bear as tightly as possible, to prevent being thrown. He instinctively reached for his knife in his belt and thrust it into the throat of the bear and with a slicing motion silenced the horrendous roars of the animal almost immediately.

A short time later, the bear fell to the ground with a thud. Robert slowly climbed off its back, and with fatigue oozing from every pore, fell exhausted to the ground beside the bloody body of Flying Eagle.

The chief, now with his own knife drawn, moved curiously forward to where the bear lay. After assuring himself the animal was in the final stages of dying, he summoned Running Deer to the two men lying motionless alongside the now quieted bear.

Running Deer immediately went to work inspecting Flying Eagle's wounds. He was alive, but a total bloody mass of broken bones, with his scalp nearly torn off. It hung loosely off the side of his head, remaining attached only by one ear.

She set about cleaning his wounds with the healing water from the magical pool nearby. It was immediately obvious that his wounds were very serious and he could not walk the few miles back to the village and must be transported on a travois. Robert, having regained his breath, understood it was up to him to make the necessary travois.

After soaking his head in the pool, he set off into the trees nearby, seeking the few long poles that would be required. He had been gone but a few minutes when he encountered the mate of the bear he had just killed. He spotted the animal before it spotted him, and in anticipation of an attack, jumped on top of a fallen tree and stood there quietly waiting.

The mate turned in Robert's direction, as if the wind had just changed directions and had carried Robert's scent into her large nostrils. As she started to charge, Robert raised himself up higher on the log, stretched his arms to the sky, and began waving them frantically. At the same time, he let out a loud, long, shrill scream that frightened both the chief and Running

Deer, who were just out of sight but a short distance away. As they quickly followed the scream, they saw Robert on the log acting like a crazy man. A further glance offered a view of a large bear's rear end as it vanished into the forest on the far side of Robert. It was obvious that Robert had frightened the bear away with his crazy antics.

The travois was made without further delay and Flying Eagle was taken back to the village. As they reached the outskirts of the village, the tribe was out in full welcome and with inquisitive questions about what had happened. Apparently, Robert's screams had carried all the way through the quiet forest, back to the village. The full story was relayed and retold many times during the rest of the day and around the evening campfire.

Running Deer and Robert set about to do what they could to repair Flying Eagles' wounds. Had Robert been back at his home in Mormon country, he would have had the things necessary to begin. Here, he had to improvise.

With that realization, he sent two of the squaws to gather some yucca needles and two other squaws to bring him some prickly cactus from just outside the village. When they arrived back, he had them strip the upper yucca growth from the extruding sharp point of the yucca and gently pound the remaining material until a strong single thread appeared and hung from the sharp needlepoint. With some further adjustments, Robert knew with six or eight such needles and thread, he would be able to proceed with his surgery and sew Flying Eagles' scalp back on the top of his head.

Robert applied a jelly like ointment, prepared from the inside pulp of the cactus, to the closure where the two flaps of skin came together. He reasoned this would help prevent infection and speed healing. During the entire operation, Running Deer watched Robert's precision closely, and her alertness was rewarding to Robert, as he quickly understood that she was absorbing this new information for possible future use.

That evening, during the Thanksgiving dances that were being done in recognition of Flying Eagle's survival, the chief arose from the teepee where Flying Eagle was recovering and approached the group. The dancing stopped and the chief spoke in low tones as he beckoned Robert to come forward. At first, Robert remained uncomfortably still. Then, with a quick snap of his thick shoulders, he moved forward as ordered.

The chief raised a ceremonial colored feather, and placing it on Robert's head, announced that he had earned the Indian name, "Killing Bear", for his bravery and quickness of thought, and as "Medicine Man", for bringing Flying Eagle back from most certain death.

With a nod from the chief, Running Deer took Killing Bear by the hand into the center of the circle around the fire. Running Deer retreated and Robert stood alone on the stage, drinking in the adoration of the tribe. As the drums again started with a new rhythm, Running Deer led Killing Bear in a celebration dance, along with the whoops and hollers of the Indians. Robert would not soon forget this honor that had been bestowed upon him.

As the fire died and the night became still, Robert looked to the heavens in thanks, and was immediately reminded of the many times he had done this with Elizabeth at his side, in long years past. It was somewhat of a shock back into reality for him, since such thoughts of Elizabeth and his sons had not entered his mind since before the massacre.

He had a restless sleep that night, and one that was interrupted frequently with pleasant, yet clouded and disturbing thoughts of his family back home in Council Bluffs. Memories were returning in full force. Both good and bad!!!

He had had the presence of mind to sew Flying Eagles' scalp back on as best he could under the primitive conditions available. Robert was satisfied Flying Eagle would recover with rest and care as he himself had previously received. However, like his own, Flying Eagle's scars would remain as an outward reminder of his close brush with death.

Chapter 29

Increasing Thoughts of Home......

Fall 1858/Spring 1859

Robert, or Killing Bear as he became known fondly within the tribe, was sought out by the young braves to accompany them on their various hunts as the tribe began preparing for winter. On one such hunt, the Indians came upon a small group of white traders. Robert was somewhat reluctant to approach them for fear they had connections with the Mormons and may recognize him as the sole adult survivor of the massacre, now but a year before. In discussion with his Indian braves, they agreed, even though he now appeared much like any other brave of the tribe that they would shield him from the trappers eyes until it could be determined if they were friend or foe.

A short time later, Robert was in full discussion with the trappers. "You have guns. We have beaver pelts and buffalo skins." It was during this encounter that Robert taught the Indians how to truly bargain with the "White man". At first, the trappers were sure that they would be able to make trades in their favor. However, as time went on and the afternoon shadows began to darken, the trade began to favor the Indians because of Robert's strong understanding of the pelts values.

The trade agreement was reached when the trappers finally were willing to give up a couple of extra rifles and powder for the pelts and skins offered. With Robert's encouragement, they had finally recognized that their trapping season would soon be over for the year, and with the weather changing, this presented a great opportunity to return home with their summer harvest truly overflowing.

The Indians returned to the village with five rifles and plenty of powder to last until the next opportunity presented itself. With rifle in hand, and much to the delight of the other Indian braves, Robert had been successful in bringing down two elk, a buck deer, and a number of other smaller animals.

In discussion with the chief, Robert selected five of the tribe's best braves to teach the use of the rifle, so that come spring they would be able to hunt on their own.

The 'trainees" were eager to learn and were truly fast learners. Before the second heavy snowfall, the selected braves were proficient in both their shooting and safety skills. Robert was more than pleased with their progress and felt somewhat content that he had been able to keep his promise to himself to "pay the tribe back" for their courtesies and vigilance during his recovery.

The winter months came on fast and were more severe than others Robert recalled. They also seemed longer. Perhaps his almost continuous thoughts on Elizabeth and "Home" made the winter both stronger and longer. Many times he would be found, by himself, outside the warm teepee with only his buckskin pants on, hoping the wind and falling snow would take away the brooding hurt he was feeling. At other times, his mind just seemed to drift in and out of various fuzzy hazes.

One night, sitting in the teepee with Running Deer at his side, his mind was recalling his and Elizabeth's "adventures" and dreams of ten or twelve years ago. As he stared into the fading fire, he made a meaningless wave with his hand that caused the ashes of the fire to be stirred. With another wave of his hand, he thought to himself how the ashes of the dying fire resembled the ashes of his dreams.

With a rush of bitter remembrances, he turned swiftly and silently from the fire, his heart literally broken. He went outside the teepee to explore the heavens with the questions that had been haunting him the past year or so.

"Why?? Why me??? Why has the west treated me so cruelly???" "Oh, Elizabeth, dear Elizabeth, I miss you so. I wish you were here!"

Chapter 30

The Return to Reality......Summer 1859

Both Robert's physical strength and his clouded memory were returning to something approaching normal. With his continual thoughts of Elizabeth and his three boys during the long winter and spring months, he began to think of various plans to leave this Indian life behind and return to the life he began to remember. For the first time in over two years, he experienced the wonderful sense of going home, to return and pick up the strings of time. He let out a long exhalation of relief at the thought.

He spent the last few waning weeks of spring in a state of controlled excitement. This inward excitement was only tempered by the thought of having to announce his intentions to the tribe, and in particular, to Running Deer.

It was two nights later that he found the courage to share his thoughts with Running Deer. With a quick intake of breath like someone about to plunge into icy water, he began. She sat there motionless, as if fastened to the side of the teepee. For a long period of time, she sat quietly, contemplating what she had just been told. Her whole body tightened and she took a deep breath. She had the quiet air of a squaw taught by her Indian background that the man had the authority. With a rare form of public expression, Running Deer warmly approached Robert with sad and downcast eyes, expressive of some deep down understanding, as if to accept that this day was to come.

That night, in their teepee, her desire seemed more primitive and exciting than at any previous time. Her dark body glowed warm and welcoming on the deerskins a few short steps away. Wordlessly, he slowly and purposely approached her and soon felt the raw warmth of her skin beneath his fingertips. He felt his body and his willpower slip quickly away. This was a magical night for them both. As morning came, Running Deer told Robert that she had the unusual light feeling of a bird dancing on shafts of air. Robert shared similar feelings, but could not bring himself to express them in such poetic terms.

Soon the entire village knew of his desire to leave their presence. No anger was shown by any member of the tribe. Robert had truly become an integral and accepted member of the tribe. He had learned it was not uncommon for honored braves to leave the tribe in search of their own horizon on the distant side of the mountain or beyond the great hunting ground. Nonetheless, such a reaction was not as Robert had expected and he scolded himself for thinking otherwise. He reminded himself that Indian culture is much different from that of the white man. Such thoughts further saddened him about his pending departure. His past almost two years with the Indians had been heart warming and had given him a fundamental appreciation of reality itself.

With the decision made and other troubling thoughts now behind him, his mind was set on how he would find his way home. His days were dull and he sat thinking for hour upon hour on a rock ledge at the edge of the village, which overlooked the valley below. His mind went over and over the same thoughts until it was ready to burst. He waited for the gentle winds, flowing up from the valley below to cleanse his mind before returning to the heart of the village.

The chief had watched Robert a few days and knew almost intuitively the demon thoughts that must be clouding his head. On one of Robert's returns from the rock ledge, the chief approached him and drew him into conversation. Until the evening fires were burning brightly, the two talked. The chief simplified and cleared the way for Robert's departure.

The chief would send Robert with various guides to the friendly Indian villages to the south to avoid any unnecessary contact with the Mormons that had done Robert so wrong.

Robert would pass from tribe to tribe as he moved further south and east toward the rising sun in the direction he needed to go. The various guides would lead him until they came to a white settlement or a group of trappers, far from further danger or discovery. The chief told him that the Indian scouts knew of many trails going in the direction Robert must take.

While Robert had learned much about trails during his life with the tribe, and he had learned one set of hoofs or pair of feet can find, but not make a path; that it is the repetition of hoofs or moccasins of the Red Man going in the same direction that beats the earth into a path leading to a watering hole or continuing forward as the main trail.

Robert welcomed the chief's thoughts of providing guides along the way, since he had not learned to read all the stories and signs told by the different trails.

The chief told Robert he knew from his youth of one such trail that led farther to the east than he had ever been. He had been told that a good portion of the trail followed natural channels and had become used by many of the trappers and traders who for years had frequently visited the various tribes. These trappers and traders had spoken of large "white" settlements much further toward the rising sun.

Many of Robert's trepidations of his return home were put as ease with this discussion with the chief and he willingly accepted the offered help.

Chapter 31

Starting the trip Home...

Late Summer 1859

Now with the help from the chief, Robert wanted to leave as quickly as possible for his return to Elizabeth. He knew that going a southern route; he most likely would have better weather and easier travel during the fall and winter months.

After his final farewell feast and goodbyes, he took his meager possessions, one rifle and two pairs of moccasins that Running Deer had made for his travels. He left with his guides early one morning before the village was stirring. With a few warning barks from some of the ever watchful dogs, they left the village undetected.

It was not long before they left the trails Robert knew well and moved quickly further south. Robert paused abruptly on a small rise overlooking a long valley below. He recognized the valley as Mountain Meadows, where his dream had come to an abrupt end two summers previously. With a deep sigh, he put the memories behind him and quickly caught up with his guides. It was not long afterwards that they reached the edge of the mountains and the forest they had been traveling through for the past three days.

They spent the night in an Indian village on the low hills just above the brown grass covered prairie, which lay below, as if a carpet of desolation. He was thankful for his guides.

He had been welcomed into this new tribe with a small feast and they truly seemed happy to be following the wishes of the chief who had sent him to them. All of his needs were carefully handled. Robert was mentally captured by this unusual and unexpected welcome by another tribe of which he knew little. His new guides were presented and it was agreed they would depart early the next morning.

They followed one monotonous trail, which only lead to another, yet wider trail, as they continued to move further and further south into country that was unknown to Robert. About noon the second day, his new guides abruptly turned on a much wider trail to the east. This trail had distinct markings of wagon wheels. Other than stops at the frequent water holes along the way, Robert and his Indian guides kept moving.

On the third day of their travels, they came over the crest of a small hill and his alert guides' motioned caution. They all fell to the ground and slowly crawled to the crest of the hill where they could secretly peer at what had caused their caution. In the small water filled ravine, they saw something that caused the two Indians to immediately slide back down the small hill seeking safety. They were astonished at Robert's bravery, as he stayed to further observe whatever had made the Indian guides so apparently fearful.

While Robert had never seen anything like this before, he knew from his university studies that such things did exist in the world. What they were doing here in this desolate place caused him pause, until he recalled it seemed a normal setting for such beasts.

He motioned to his guides to return. Somewhat reluctantly, they did so, since they saw no fear in Robert. With some knowledge of their particular language, Robert explained that what they were seeing were merely some unusual and unique animals seeking water.

As they silently watched with fascination, two white men approached the animals and began to lead them out of the ravine and into a campsite that the Indian guides and Robert had previously totally missed.

They continued to watch, and it became apparent that these white men were merely traders passing through with their wares. After watching them for perhaps another hour, Robert decided that an encounter with them would be safe.

He told the two guides to stay concealed while he approached the traders, and with that, he went back down the hill to approach them from a different direction. He walked into the ravine where the strange animals had been watering, and moved out of the ravine in the direction of the traders' campsite.

Upon seeing Robert emerge from the ravine, the trappers immediately reached for their rifles. In an instant, Robert realized that his appearance was that of an Indian and he must do something quickly to keep from being shot dead.

He slowly raised his hand, palm out in the universal sign of peace. At the same time, he spoke an English greeting that the trappers would immediately recognize as coming from one of their own. "What are you fellows doing way out here in the middle of nowhere?" asked Robert, in his recently seldom used English voice.

The two traders were immediately put at ease, and Robert proceeded into their camp. A short time later, Robert motioned and speaking with his Indian tongue, called his two guides to join him.

Cautiously, they approached, carefully watching both the traders and the unusual huge beasts now eating some grass at the edge of the campsite.

As Robert explained that these Indians were his guides, leading him out of the wilderness, the traders seemed anxious to welcome them into their midst. While they traded with many Indians out here in the wilderness, it was always wise to not trust anyone you came across, red or white man, until you were sure of the safety of the meeting.

The late afternoon was spent in discussion around the campfire. The Indians sat slightly off to one side by themselves. It was at this point that Robert asked the traders how they had come to have the camels.

They related that they had found them a year before, wandering around the prairie, and had just taken possession of them. They since learned that a General Biele of the U.S. Calvary, had over the previous two years, brought over one hundred camels to this part of the country from northern Africa. He had set up a Camel Corp to help protect the movement of travelers on the trails to the gold field of California. The General apparently had studied the camel, became enthusiastic, and felt these animals were well suited for this desert country. Others, including the famous frontier guide, Kit Carson, were not convinced and the project was dropped, with the animals turned loose.

Robert asked if he and the Indian guides could approach the animals. With laughter in their voices, the traders gave their blessings.

The strange scent of the Indians excited the camels, almost as much as the scent of the camels caused Robert and the Indians' nostrils to flair. When one on the camels spit at them as they gathered near his front quarters for a closer look, they immediately and shockingly made their retreat.

That night the traders shared some firewater with their three guests. Shortly, the Indians were staggering off over the hill to spend the night, while Robert had his second fill. Strangely, it tasted much like the "Tarantula juice" with which he had previously been familiar. It even somewhat resembled the spit they had earlier received from the camel.

As the drinking continued and as the fire heated the traders' bodies and clothing, Robert could not decide which seemed worse, the smell of the camels or that of the traders. As he dozed off to sleep, he promised himself to make that important decision in the morning.

Robert awoke to the smell of coffee, one he had not smelled for a long, long time. The same smell had attracted the two Indians who had spent the night in the nearby ravine. Robert's call to them to come for food produced immediate results.

After eating, the Indians, noting Robert was now with his own kind, announced they would take their leave and return to their village. With an Indian handshake of thanks with each of them, Robert sent them on their way. They honored their own chief and Robert's chief by locating a continuation of his journey home that assured his safety.

Robert watched until they disappeared from sight and thought to himself, "What tales they would be telling their tribe about the strange animals they had been with", and Robert further wondered if they would be believed.

Shortly afterward, the traders packed up and loaded the camels with what Robert thought were huge loads of furs and other trade goods, which they had received from trading with the Indians during the summer months. They set off, moving east and toward the settlements that lay beyond the great river that they had mentioned to Robert.

Each night around the campfire, they welcomed Robert's company and stories of his adventures, and he welcomed the thought that each day's travels had brought him closer to his reunion with Elizabeth and his boys.

Chapter 32

Civilization..... Fall 1859

After crossing the Great River at Lee's Ferry, the traders left Robert for their own trip down river and to their own winter homes.

Many Emigrant wagons had just started passing over this newly established "Middle Route" to the California gold fields. It was the shortest route, mostly level and reportedly that only once did a wagon have to double team during the entire distance. It was well watered, with the greatest distance without water but twenty miles or a day's travel. It passed through a country abounding in game and little infected with hostile Indians. Those encountered were most likely Zuni and somewhat more friendly with the whites passing through.

This "Middle Trail", Robert learned, led eastward across a vast desert to a place called Santa Fe. Robert had previously heard of the Santa Fe Trail and became anxious to move on.

The main problem was that most travelers were heading west to California, with few returning eastwardly. He would have to bide his time at Lee's Ferry until he could locate a wagon going East; he knew he needed the time, anyway, to adjust back into the white man's way of life.

He willingly helped with the ferry crossings for a number of weeks. For his efforts he was given various pieces of clothing most which fit very poorly. He needed to replace his buckskin Indian garb that made him conspicuous and now, sadly, even a bit self conscious.

He did not discuss his past adventures with anyone, still somewhat fearful that his survival from the massacre would be discovered, with dire consequences. He learned that word of the massacre had reached public awareness across the entire continent, and numerous investigations were now taking place within all Mormon communities. Even this far from where the deed had been done, he was alert to other Mormon communities that had recently sprung up in the general vicinity of where he now found himself. This made him fearful he would be recognized, since he had been so well known through the entire Great Basin Mormon settlements, some of whom may have migrated this far south.

One of the wagons passing though to the west gave him pair of boots to replace his now well warn moccasins. The next day, he located a couple of wagons returning eastward. In fact, the traders with the camels had visited with these two men and had helped them bury the third man of the group a few weeks ago. They had told the men of the wagon to be on the lookout for Robert and give him any help they could.

It was like a gift from Heaven. The two men of the wagon needed a replacement for the man they had lost, and they were moving in the right direction for Robert. They asked little of why Robert appeared to be running from someone or something. They accepted him for just what he seemed to be......A simple, yet desperate craggy loner.

During the few days they rested their team at Lee's Ferry, they became better acquainted with Robert and he with them. He learned their names were Jake Roggy and Mathew Diehl. Cautiously, he admitted to them that he was indeed running away from a terrible experience and must be shielded from sight, should new danger present itself. With no further explanation from Robert, they agreed to honor his caution if and when it might occur.

Robert quickly proved his value to his new acquaintances by guiding them in the purchase of the necessary horses to replace those they had recently lost. Local horses were hard to come by and those that were available left something to be desired. Robert had good horse sense and made the selection of the best there was to offer. Additionally, his previous trading experience and negotiating skills saved a great deal of hard cash for his new "bosses".

One midday, as Robert was finishing his daily work routine of helping with the ferry crossing, he recognized a number of men on a Mormon wagon train, waiting for their turn to make the eastern return crossing of the river. Upon recognizing some of the travelers as old acquaintances, his instincts quickly took over and he hid from sight on the overhang of the raft, amongst the rigging. He remained there during the entire return crossing and until the two wagons and his previous Mormon friends had taken their wagons and their families and disappeared from sight.

Roberts new "bosses" observed Robert as he freed himself from the rigging of the underside of the raft and quickly approached him to offer assistance. He told them he must seek immediate safety, away from the people on the two wagons that had just arrived from the other side of the river. Without further questions, they put Robert in the bottom of their wagon and covered him with various items to conceal him fully.

That night, Robert confided in them that the Mormon men he had seen were old friends who had done him an injustice on behalf of the Church and were now probably seeking to establish a new Mormon settlement somewhere in the territory east of Lee's Ferry.

With this news, his two new friends prepared a fake bottom in one of the wagons with sufficient room to conceal Robert should the occasion arise. This was done voluntarily, again with no questions asked. That night, it was decided that it would be best they leave Lee's Ferry the next morning.

With Robert concealed in the fake bottom of the wagon, they set off to the east shortly after breakfast. As luck would have it, only a few miles out of Lee's Ferry, they intersected the path of the Mormon families Robert had been trying to avoid. Robert practically held his breath as he peered out between the cracks of the wagon bed at his murderous "friends" of two years previous. As Jake and Mathew exchanged pleasantries with the Mormons, Robert was listening carefully for any words that may betray his concealed presence.

He began to wonder if he was going completely mad or just becoming more paranoid. He lay in his concealed area for the next six hours, as the Mormon wagons joined with the traders as they all moved eastward. As the daylight began to fade, the Mormon wagons turned south and disappeared over some distant hills.

As Robert emerged from his daylong hiding place, he thanked his benefactors and then quickly began to fix the evening meal. However, it was not until four or five days later, that he really began to feel free of any concern or retribution from the Mormons. He hoped also that these feelings were permanent and that he had finally left his past where it belonged… in the past.

Chapter 33

The Zuni Trail…….

As they continued moving east, they began meeting differently dressed Indians that seemed friendly and would approach them. Robert again proved his value with these encounters. He had a lot of respect for the Indian manners and had learned to always treat new tribes with some apprehension. He had little fear of them and always greeted them with a welcoming sign. Such greetings amongst the various Indian tribes were customary, but such greetings coming from a "white man" were most unusual and caused much interest amongst the Indians. They wanted to learn more of this "white man".

Many times a small group of Indians would stay for an evening meal and further discussion with Robert and his friends. Through these visits, it was learned that earlier traders had named this trail the Zuni Trail after the friendly Indians that lived in the area. The trail combined the directness of good traveling conditions toward Santa Fe with comparative freedom from savage attack. From other travelers, they learned that the trail was now called Cooke's Wagon Road and was abounding in game.

Robert became the most successful hunter and fresh food provider by applying the skills he had learned during his time with the Pah-Vantes.

The closer they got to Santa Fe, the more Robert began to have recurring wistful thoughts. His shoulders would droop and his gait would slow. He walked in a state of loneliness to his bedroll each night. His feeling for Elizabeth grew stronger and stronger with each passing day. A bitter rush of remembrances of his broken dreams would bring him back to the twilight world of half alive.

The boredom of the endless prairie and his impatience, were beginning to take its toll on Robert. Having survived on excitement, he knew he now must adjust to life in a more civilized world.

Robert's time in the frontier town of Santa Fe was rather short-lived. He found it rather rambunctious and lacking in the peace and quiet he had known, but at the same time, he had to agree, it seemed to have a glamorous and exciting mystique. However, nothing could relieve Robert from his feeling of uneasiness and his restlessness for fresh new horizons.

Upon saying his goodbyes to Jake and Mathew, he was given one of the horses that he had helped them purchase in Lee's Ferry. This was totally unexpected but certainly most welcome and necessary for the continuation of his travels "Home".

After having spent only four days in Santa Fe, and now with his own horse, he was ready to leave. He hoped to leave the next day with a small group of men who where making their way to the newly discovered gold fields in the Colorado territory.

Chapter 34

Into The Kansas Territory......Fall 1859

While weather was of some concern to Robert it was overcome by his ever growing desire to reach "Home" and Elizabeth as soon as possible. His new companions had similar feelings. They were anxious to reach the newly discovered gold fields of Colorado and stake out their claims to new fortunes.

They began to gather their necessary provisions and agreed to leave before the weeks end. Discussions followed as to the best, quickest and safest route to take.....one somewhat shorter "cutoff" trail due north through the now friendly Indian pueblo of Taos, or stay on the Santa Fe trail moving north east to Fort Union, and beyond towards Bent's Fort.

They welcomed Robert's knowledge of the wilds of the west and listened intensely as he related the possible harshness and cruelty of the western frontier's winters. After a night of quite a number of Tarantula drinks, they decided the smartest route to take, while a bit longer, would be the safest and the best insurance against any problems, weather or otherwise, that they might incur.

The small group left as planned and found the trip slower than anticipated due to the pack horses that they had brought along to carry all their provisions. Robert, on the other hand, had only his horse, his saddle, his gun and his bedroll. Robert's impatience frequently showed, with both the delays and with their continual talk of how they would spend their new wealth upon striking it rich. It seemed they could talk about nothing else. Robert had well learned that dreams could be turned to dust in a twinkle of the eye and stayed completely out of their discussions and their dreams of wealth.

They stopped at Fort Union overnight. Before leaving the following morning, they discussed the trail east with a number of men from the wagon train that had arrived the night before, just as they had. No problems had been encountered anywhere along the trail from Bent's Fort.

They found this to be true as they moved eastward on the now well established Santa Fe Trail. When they reached a point about five days travel out from Bent's Fort, they took a trail pointing due north along the eastern edge of high mountains that could be seen further west.

Luckily, the heavy snows held off, at least on the part of the prairie they were traveling. Looking to the west each morning, they observed new snow that had capped the mountains that rose majestically into the vivid blue sky.

Ten days later, when they reached a river junction and a small community called Colorado City, the group started to split up. This community had been established within a day's travel of the highest capped mountain peak any of them had ever seen. A number in the group immediately recognized it as the area they had heard about and where their new adventure was to begin. They had reached their destination..... "Pikes Peak or Bust".

As part of the group debated whether to move on or stay and test their luck in these mountains, Robert made up his mind immediately.

He learned the trail they had been following and that continued on north, had been establish the year before by two men by the names of Oliver Loving and John Durkee. Loving had driven the first herd of Texas longhorns north from Texas in 1858 to supply food for the newly discovered gold fields. Two other men, Chisholm and Goodnight, had followed suit, and were now also supplying cattle to the hungry gold searchers.

Robert learned that Chisholm and a large herd of Texas longhorns had passed through the area just days before and thought to himself, if he left immediately he may catch up to the cattle drive and find work.

Two days later, after a short discussion with Chisholm himself, he was riding drag at the rear of the herd and rounding up strays. This slowed his travels north, but he realized he also needed money to continue his trip "Home", and the herd was moving in the direction he needed to go.

He enjoyed rounding up the animals that strayed from the main herd. It took him off the beaten trail into hills and valleys of the eastern prairie he would not otherwise have seen. Sometimes, his search would take him miles off the main trail. He observed how fertile the land had become and understood why the cattle strayed, seeking the new high grasses, they seemed to sense or smell. Grass as far as the eye could see.

At one point, the grass disappeared into rather heavy wooded low hills covered with pine trees, producing a "Black Forest". This area was reminiscent of the area he had loved but left along with Running Deer and his other Indian friends above Mountain Meadows. The main difference was the huge butte, or protruding rock formation, rising out of the rolling prairie, and appeared from a distance, to be a huge castle.

The weather changed quickly and Robert found himself stranded to the east of this castle formation and away from the main herd and the safety of the camp. He sought refuge in the "Black Forest" area he had previously observed. He had found four longhorns before the snow became so thick he could search no further. He placed them in a ravine just below the place in the forest where he had found some shelter for himself.

The snow did not let up for two days, and his grub that he had in his saddlebags was all but gone. He had to find some food for himself and for the rescued longhorns.

He could not go far in the deep snow that had fallen but knew if any thing was to be found it would be on the lee side of the castle rock. Only a short distance away from his own camping site he discovered a group of six Indian teepees that were also detained by the storm. Robert approached the teepees tentatively and was all the way into the center of the teepee camp before he saw anyone. When two young braves jumped out of a nearby teepee, Robert was surprised, but recovered his composure quickly and greeted them with the usual Indian greeting he knew so well. With an Indian yell, young braves had alerted the remainder of the camp of this intruder.

Soon, inquisitive Indians, undoubtedly wondering from where this white man had come, surrounded Robert. Robert listened closely to the jabbering going on around him and recognized some of the words that were being spoken. His mind flashed back to Hart's Bluff, Elizabeth and the young Indian girl they had taken in and from whom he had learned some Indian language.

Using both sign language and the Pawnee and Ute languages he remembered, he felt he gave a persuasive account of who he was and why he was wandering around in the heavy snow.

After a little further discussion, Robert was welcomed into one of the teepees for warmth and to share some of their meager remaining food. While sitting in the circle around the small fire in the center of the teepee, Robert had many flashbacks of earlier episodes in his life. As the fire began to die and the embers yet remained, Robert sat motionless and recalled the event that had turned his dreams to ashes. As his consciousness returned, his first thoughts were of Elizabeth, and to both his own amazement and that of the seated Indians, he realized he was speaking aloud.

The next few days were spent with the Indians, feasting on one of the longhorns Robert had provided.

The weather again changed quickly, taking with the change most of the snow that had fallen. It was time for Robert to move on. He knew the main herd would not be far ahead, since they, too, would have been stopped by the heavy snowfall.

He was not wrong, and he found them just to the west of the castle rock the late afternoon of the day he left the Indians. The cowboys were surprised to see him and had all but written him off as lost to the storm. Chisholm was particularly pleased to see that he had brought back a total of seven cattle, three of which Robert had added to his collection on the way back to the main herd.

The rest of the forty miles to the final destination at the confluence of Cherry Creek and the South Platte River, was uneventful and took them just five days.

On one side of the river was Denver City, named after the Governor of the Kansas territory of which this area was now a part. On the other side was Auraria, the first permanent settlement in the area. It was called Auraria, from the Latin word for gold and had been so named by it founder, a man named Russell.

The entire settlement was nothing to truly speak of, other than to say that just five days after the snowstorm Robert found it nothing more than a muddy, dirty crossroads of loud and rowdy gold seekers.

Chapter 35

Wintering in Denver City, Kansas Territory

... Late 1859

With the experience of the snow at Castle Butte, and in talking to recent arrivals from the east, Robert felt it best to remain in the area for the next few months. He quickly found a job with the only butcher in Denver City and was sure in the weeks to come that he would be butchering many of the animals he had just drove in with Chisholm. He had no interest in seeking gold. His only interest was to leave for Elizabeth and home at the first sign of good weather.

Robert, always curious, used his time in Denver City to learn about the area and the people that made up the settlement. He became a close "drinking" friend of the blacksmith who had arrived the year before from the Santa Fe area. He was a big, burly man with a very loud voice that had given him the nickname "Noisy Tom". His real name was Tom Pollock.

Other information Robert gathered came from the areas only newspaper, which was first published just a few months before his arrival. An intellectual man named Byers owned the paper and named it *The Rocky Mountain News*. The *News* puffed Denver as the pre-ordained metropolis of the Rockies, even imagining river traffic for the high, dry city on the shallow South Platte. Much of the news was aimed at Omaha, Council Bluffs, and other cities filled with investors, capital, and potential emigrants. Byers called Denver the steamboat hub of the Rockies. Noting that water traffic had made major cities out of New Orleans, St. Louis, and other river towns, Byers launched a "Shipping News" department. On September 10, 1859, the *News* announced in a "Boat Departures" column: "The Scow, Arapahoe", was leaving for New Orleans, laden with passengers and freight."

Robert quickly discounted the idea that this new settlement of Denver would ever become a major river town, but was intrigued with the man who thought so, especially when he learned that he had been a prime mover in Omaha, an area Robert had known well, twelve years previously. Robert sought out William Byers and had no difficulty recognizing him from his fancy dress and clean cut appearance. Such appearances stood out in this otherwise rough, uncultured frontier town. During the winter months, the two had many conversations concerning how Omaha and Council Bluffs had grown and what similarities were possible in the future of this new frontier settlement.

While others were gambling on gold, Robert and other adventuresome men mined the miners, relieving them of whatever wealth they might have found up in the hills. They gambled with cards and dice, for most anything of value. They bet on everything from dogfights to snowfall. This kept money flowing throughout the settlement and many businesses alive during the slow winter months.

In the early spring of 1860, Robert had had more than enough of this bustling town with boozers and losers. He had saved his money and was anxious to continue his journey home at the first indication of good weather.

He did not have long to wait. The first stage to arrive from the east in months had just pulled in and reported no major problems during their journey. Upon receiving that news, Robert sought out his friend "Noisy" Tom Pollock to tell him he was leaving. He found him surrounded by a group of businessmen, including the paper's publisher, William Byers.

Standing on the outer fringes of the gathering, Robert listened closely as the businessmen were trying to obtain "Noisy" Tom's commitment to become the first marshal of the newly formed Denver City. After a great deal of further discussion, Tom somewhat reluctantly agreed to serve. Robert immediately knew the decision was the right one and that Tom was well suited for the job.

Many in the group gathered at the Apollo Hall, the local saloon, to celebrate their choice and Tom's agreement. Robert joined in the celebration with glee. By 8:00 pm, the group finally thinned. Only Tom and Robert remained to celebrate Robert's own decision to continue his journey home to Elizabeth.

Chapter 36

Home ... But a Few Weeks More.......

Early Spring 1860

The last spring snow had melted in the warmth of the day. Robert knew it was now time to leave.

The eastward trail to the northeast from Denver City, and which joined the Oregon Trail, was now well marked by previous passing gold seekers. In addition, various small settlements had sprung up along the way making travel much safer and easier. With this knowledge, Robert set off by himself on the horse that his friends in Santa Fe had given him, and a map of the various settlements that he had obtained from another frequent patron of the Apollo Hall saloon.

As Robert passed through the various settlements, he would cross them off the map. The more he checked off, the faster the next one seemed to appear in his sight. He checked off settlement names mostly unfamiliar to him; Pierson's, Fort Lupton, Big Bend, Eagle's Nest, Bijou Creek, Beaver Cheek, Kelley's, Fort Wicked, Valley, Dennison's, Spring Hill, and Antelope. The next settlement name he was to check off, Julesburg, told him he was drawing very near to the Oregon Trail and that Fort Kearny would be next.

Upon reaching Fort Kearny, his thoughts turned to his original trip through the area and how the wagon train would have welcomed the safety and conveniences of what now had become a very impressive and extensive fort. When he had first passed through, the fort had only been established in the spring of that year and had offered very little in the way of supplies or help, and the soldiers were a most unsoldierly looking lot. They were unshaven and had patched uniforms and nothing good to say to the travellers. All Robert could think was "Progress!"

He crossed the river as he left the Fort to connect to the portion of the Oregon Trail leading to Council Bluffs. Travelling as he was, he knew he would be in Elizabeth's arms in just over a week. Such thoughts brought renewed strength and determination to him to reach his destination quickly. However, as such thoughts abated, Robert felt an unusual feeling of apprehension and a faint, though distant, nervous anxiety. It was a frightening feeling and one he could not understand, and it sent his mind whirling.

The next days of his travels brought an ever-increasing obsessive sense of everything going wrong. At the end of each days travel, as he drew ever closer to his home in Council Bluffs, his evenings and his sleep developed a chopped, chaotic tempo that infected all his hours. He began to develop a terrible sense of failure and the humiliation that was sure to follow.

In spite of his resolve, inexorably his mind returned to his past, allowing his subconscious to surface. He had walked and lived on the knife-edge of danger and had survived. Yet now he worried that his experiences and his past occasional loss of memory were beginning to make their mark and take their full toll.

Robert tried to shake these feelings and thoughts. His brain dimly tried to comb out the tangles of the past, but with more difficulty than he had ever before experienced. He felt as if he were going mad.

In the few wakening moments of reality, with some inkling of the sane mind of a physician, he knew the stress and tension that had built up over his return home was the instigator of his new mental anguish. He rationalized that his only cure was to expedite his trip into Elizabeth's arms.

However, little helped him as his mind tumbled through all the names, faces and events of the past twelve years and the adventurous anticipation of his younger days. Memories opened before him as if a curtain had been ripped, making his mind bulge with unanswered questions.

Finally, some relief came after having suffered for five days. The relief was in the form of familiar sights, places and things. He recognized the area he was now passing through as the Indian country where he had first been called to treat chief Wandulta's young son. He recalled the fear and knotting he had felt in his stomach as he had entered the Indian camp for the first time. He had somewhat of the same feeling now as he approached the western side of the river, opposite Council Bluffs and Elizabeth.

With approaching nightfall, he found himself in the largest mega metropolis he had seen since Salt Lake City. From earlier discussions with William Barnes in Denver City, Robert knew immediately that this was the new city of Omaha that he had described and which was now across the river from Council Bluffs.

Robert's heart began to beat faster and faster, as he rushed to the waters edge, seeking the barge that he hoped would take him across. His heart sunk when he learned the barge had made its last run for the day and he must wait until sun up to cross.

He stood on the riverbank and looked longingly across the river to the few flickering lights that he could see. He wondered if one belonged to the cabin that he and Elizabeth had settled into when they had first arrived in Hart's Bluff, now Council Bluff. His eyes moistened with such pleasant memories.

With some of the money he had left, he took a room for the night above one of the many saloons. Quickly, he drifted into a deep sleep, despite the noise that entered his room from the saloon below. Morning could not come soon enough for Robert.

At first light, Robert washed in the basin provided and took a long studied look at his reflection in the mirror. He had seen no mirrors for as long as he could remember. The returning view from the mirror brought him up short. "Who was this man staring back at him?", he almost asked himself aloud.

What he saw was a man with ugly scar tissue on the top of his head, a few strands of dirty soot gray, somewhat wavy hair that fell almost to his eyebrows, whiskers that covered his face like an ape, and an overall grungy-looking human being. He had a hard time recognizing the face that stared back at him.

After breakfast, he arranged for a tub bath, the first he had had in two or three years. As he soaked, he recalled this as one of the nicer things of civilized life. Upon finishing shaving, he noted the white, unbleached skin that had been uncovered for the first time in years. Shortening the length of the few strands of hair remaining on his head, he recognized how obvious and unsightly the scarring was that had been left from the Mountain Meadows scalping episode.

He set upon the remaining graying hair by applying heavy oil and combing it sideways and upward to conceal the disfiguration as best he could. The result was more like the coiffure arrangements he had seen on some of the "Fancy Dan's" he had seen in San Francisco, and determined immediately to wear his hat low and cocked to the left side to more fully cover the hideous scarring. He was somewhat sorry he had cut any of his hair in the first place.

He put on the best and cleanest clothes he had left and proceeded to the stable for his horse. The bath, whisker, and hair removal had given him a new, lighter walking gait. As his approached, his horse, the horse shied away, indicating he was not recognized. It could have been the smelly bath oil remaining on Robert's body or just plainly the smell of "Clean" that caused the horse to be so obstinate at first. He saddled and quickly rode to the river's edge, just in time to catch the next barge crossing.

Robert stood at the front of the barge, picking out known sights as they came into view. His breathing became irregular with excitement, and as the barge reached the Council Bluffs' side of the river, Robert was on his horse and the first one off.

He paused momentarily as he passed the stable and blacksmith shop of his old friend, Frank Ragland, and his Indian wife, Choovio. The stable had grown considerably and there were many horses and other activity around the area. For a moment, Robert thought he observed Choovio as she disappeared into the stable with a basket under her arm. He would have time for later visits and proceeded on his way toward his old cabin on the hill.

The "Trading Post" at the bottom of hill, owned by his and Elizabeth's best friends, had disappeared and been replaced by a much large building. The sign on the building identified it as "La Rouche General Merchandise Emporium". "Ah", thought Robert, "Louis and his wife Michelle have succeeded beyond all our dreams." As Robert rounded the road at the bottom of the hill, he had pangs in his heart concerning his own lack of success.

He reached his old cabin and observed how beautiful it was with its abundance of various spring flowers, obviously planted and cared for by Elizabeth in her love of the beauty of nature. He tied his horse to the fence post and opened the swinging gate into the yard. He stopped to carefully select a bouquet of her creations before proceeding to the front door.

With a deep breath, Robert knocked gently on the front door and waited patiently with love in his heart, flowers in his hand and a smile on his face. His heart beat faster as he heard soft footsteps approaching the door from the inside.

The door slowly creaked its opening and Robert, with his freshly picked bouquet held in front of him like a man on his first date, replied, "Mother, I'm home!"

Elizabeth took a step forward to get a closer look at the voice she had heard. Her heart began beating faster as she recognized both the voice and the Robert she had known and loved twelve years previously, and whom she thought long dead since she had not heard from in all that time.

At that moment, a young boy of perhaps five years old approached from the back of the cabin and inquisitively called out, "Momma, who is it?"

Elizabeth took a faltering step back and turned a pasty white as blood drained from her face. A small flicker of a smile rose at the edges of her mouth and then died out as her lips started to form the name "Robert", the name she had spoken so often years before.

Putting her hand to her chest, Robert's beloved Elizabeth fell dead on the doorstep of their old cabin on the hill.

The gentle morning breeze carried petals from Robert's flower bouquet over to and around Elizabeth's still body, as if to voice his own lamented thoughts of *"Broken Dreams"*...

****

*****

***

*

Story Postlude

The young boy that asked "Momma, who is it?" was Milo Slythe Jr., the son of Elizabeth and Milo Slythe Sr. Elizabeth had married Milo Slythe six or eight years prior to Robert's return home.

All letters and money promised by Robert and sent to Elizabeth with the couriers of the Church of Jesus Christ of Latter-day Saints, had either mysteriously disappeared or somehow had ceased to arrive, causing Elizabeth and all other close friends to think Robert killed or otherwise dead in the new dangerous frontier. All inquiries into the matter had gone unanswered by the Church.

Robert's three boys, George Adelbert, David and Lou, were grown young boys when Robert returned. The four lived together in Council Bluffs and were engaged in farming for a number of years after his return.

It was perhaps three to five years after Robert's return that they all left together to seek new adventures in the Colorado territory. Robert had passed through this promising new frontier on his return "Home" in 1860 and had described it to the boys as "Beautiful, Rich, Fertile and full of new opportunities".

The known facts of the lives of Robert and his three sons in Colorado are documented in "The Wood Family Chronicles", compiled by Everett Wood and first presented to the family in 1996.

DREAMS

Stir the Magic of Your Dreams to Action....

Then

"With a Heart for any Fate"
Live those Dreams to the Fullest!

180

The Author..........

Everett Wood personifies the cliché: "Play the hand that's dealt you." He believes as one ages, an exciting life can be had if one engages completely in the realities of that life and relishes those declining years with action. His writing experience began at age 75 and provided an opening to a whole new world of historical research and adventure. This coupled with his rich family heritage, has produced two novels so far, with hopes for more. A fourth generation Coloradan, he lives in Fort Collins, Colorado.